...HY THE ...D SINGS

NOTES

including
- *Life and Background*
- *Introduction to the Book*
- *List of Characters*
- *Critical Commentaries*
- *Glossaries*
- *Genealogy*
- *Maps*
- *Critical Analysis*
- *Critical Essays*
- *Selected Bibliography*

by
Mary Robinson, M.A.
University of North Carolina at Greensboro

Wiley Publishing, Inc.

CliffsNotes™ *I Know Why the Caged Bird Sings*

Published by:
Wiley Publishing, Inc.
909 Third Avenue
New York, NY 10022
www.wiley.com

CONTENTS

Centerfold—Genealogy
Pertinent maps of Arkansas and California

I KNOW WHY THE CAGED BIRD SINGS
Notes

LIFE AND BACKGROUND

Lauded as a multifaceted superstar, Maya Angelou—a tall, gap-toothed, spirited individualist who is often labeled feminist writer, African-American autobiographer, historian, lecturer, journalist, activist, filmmaker, poet, singer, actor, and storyteller—fits no single designation. She set out to whip a variety of challenges, including the language barrier, and learned French, Italian, Spanish, Serbo-Croatian, Arabic, and Fanti, a Ghanaian dialect. Her dazzling blend of talents and energies renders her uniquely suited to a variety of self-directed projects, all of which broaden and ennoble her. Her works, translated into ten languages and hitting bestseller lists on two continents, attest to an indomitable spirit. In her words, "I will not allow *anybody* to minimize my life, not *anybody*, not a living soul—nobody, no lover, no mother, no son, no boss, no President, nobody."

Childhood and Adolescence.   As she reveals in *I Know Why the Caged Bird Sings*, Maya Angelou [mah′ yuh an′ jeh loh] was born Marguerite Ann Johnson in St. Louis, Missouri, on April 4, 1928. The second child and first daughter of Bailey Johnson, a brash, insouciant Navy dietician, and Vivian Baxter Johnson, a nurse by profession and gambler by trade, Angelou acquired the first half of her pen name from her brother, Bailey Junior, whose babyish babbling transformed "my sister" into "Maya." Following her parents' divorce in 1931, Maya and Bailey, labeled on their wrists with "To Whom It May Concern," were dispatched by train from Long Beach, California, to Stamps, Arkansas, a rural Southern backwash that contrasted deeply with the citified gaiety of Maya's birthplace.

Stamps's nurturing community spirit became Maya's surrogate

family. Under the care of Momma, the children's Old South paternal grandmother, and their semi-paralyzed Uncle Willie, the children lived in the town's black quarter in the rear of the Wm. Johnson General Merchandise Store, the family-owned grocery and feed store. There they absorbed iron-clad, no-nonsense religious and moral training, punctuated by lashes with a switch from a peach tree, and reminders that the Almighty brooked no laxness and that Momma Henderson tolerated neither dirt nor backtalk. Maya's escapism from her grim, dutiful everyday life led her to classic literature, particularly white writers—Shakespeare, Kipling, Poe, Thackeray, and James Weldon Butler—and notable black authors—Paul Dunbar, Langston Hughes, W. E. B. Du Bois, and James Weldon Johnson.

Returned by her father to the Baxters' extended family in St. Louis in 1936, Maya, thoroughly indoctrinated with Momma's strictures, was reintroduced to the easy ways of the big city, where her self-absorbed mother drank and danced in gambling halls, kept company with a new man, and encouraged her babies to enjoy food, music, and other indulgences which had been in short supply in Stamps. This idyllic season in Maya's life ended abruptly after Vivian's lover, Mr. Freeman, raped Maya. To add to the emotional torture, she was forced to testify against her attacker. After her uncles murdered the rapist, the tenderhearted eight year old, refusing to speak, crept into a wounded, private world of fear and guilt.

Unsuited to the demands of an emotionally damaged child, Vivian returned Maya to Stamps, where, with Momma's guidance, she rebuilt self-esteem by cocooning herself from the outside world, reading classic literature, excelling at school, and imitating the genteel, bookish tastes of Mrs. Bertha Flowers, an old-school black Southern aristocrat who ministered to her need for pampering. Following Maya's graduation with honors from the eighth grade at Lafayette County Training School in 1940, Momma escorted her to Los Angeles, where Vivian met them and helped them move into an apartment. After Bailey joined them a month later, Momma returned to Stamps, and Maya and Bailey joined Vivian in Oakland. Later, after Vivian married Daddy Clidell Jackson, the family eventually settled in a fourteen-room house on Post Street in San Francisco's Fillmore district.

Matriculating by day at George Washington High School and in the evening at the California Labor School from 1941 to 1945, Maya, who dreamed of becoming a real estate agent, complete with brief-case (in spite of her grandmother's hopes that she would become a preacher) developed the blend of scholarship and creativity that undergirds her current success. Following a short vacation at her father's trailer in southern California and a thirty-day disappearance, she returned to her mother's care and besieged city bureaucracy for a job as San Francisco's first black streetcar conductor. Shortly after summer school graduation from Mission High, she bore a son, Clyde Bailey "Guy" Johnson, who was fathered by a neighborhood boy.

Young Womanhood. For the remainder of the 1940s, to sup-port her child, Angelou moved about California and took a variety of jobs—dancing in night clubs, cooking at a Creole cafe, removing paint at a dent and body shop, and serving as madam and sometime prosti-tute at a San Diego brothel. Terrified of arrest for her illegal activities, she hastily returned to Stamps, then Louisville, where the Army accepted, then ousted her because of her connection with the Califor-nia Labor School, which was sponsored by the Communist Party. In the interim, she eased the pain of rejection with marijuana and a new career hoofing to "Blue Flame" and "Caravan" as one half of the exotic dance duo of "Poole and Rita."

More short-term jobs followed, including fry cook in Stockton and a second short stint in prostitution. However, when Angelou became aware of Bailey's deep despair over the death of his young wife, Eunice, she returned her attention to family matters, and, in spite of his great sorrow, Bailey, concerned for the company his sister was immersed in, forced her to give up her dissolute life. A yearning to support herself drove Angelou to sell stolen clothes for a junkie, but on his advice, she stayed free of drugs, escaped the seamy life, and again sought a legitimate job.

While clerking in a record shop at the age of twenty-two, Maya met and married Tosh Angelos, a Greek-American sailor, and settled into domesticity in Los Angeles. However, beset by family and neigh-borhood disapproval of their mixed-race marriage, the relationship lasted only a few years, crumbling about the time of Momma's death. From 1954 to 1955, after a stint as exotic dancer at the Garden of Allah, Angelou left Guy in Vivian's care and toured Europe and Africa with a U.S. Department of State production of *Porgy and Bess*. Com-pelled by maternal unrest, she returned to California and settled in a houseboat commune in Sausalito to mother her son.

Career. Because petty instances of neighborhood racism continued to plague her, the respite was shortlived. Within the year, with impetus from black poet John Oliver Killens, Angelou, eager to polish her writing skills, pushed on to New York and allied herself with the Harlem Writers Guild in the late 50s. Years of private music and drama training and dance classes with Martha Graham, Pearl Primus, and Ann Halprin prepared her well for a career. Searching for outlets for her talents in the 1950s, she danced and sang calypso and blues at San Francisco's Purple Onion, New York's Village Vanguard, and Chicago's Mr. Kelly's. In the 1960s, she sang at Harlem's Apollo Theatre and appeared in off-Broadway New York theatrical productions, including *Heatwave* and Jean Genet's *The Blacks.* Spurred by civil rights gains, she joined talents with comedian Godfrey Cambridge and wrote and produced *Cabaret for Freedom,* which epitomized a time of change when black performers and writers were receiving salaries and notoriety equivalent to their talents.

Sharing a common-law marriage with Vusumzi Make [mah' kay], a suave South African anti-apartheid leader from Johannesburg, in 1961, Angelou transported her interest and enthusiasm to a colony of black American expatriates in Egypt. As Madame Make, she lived in a milieu where her chocolate brown skin and nappy hair were accepted as "correct and normal." Although the relationship dissolved after she grew tired of her mate's patriarchal attitudes, mismanagement of money, and infidelities, she remained in Africa and for two years served as the first female editor of the *Arab Observer*, a Cairo news weekly. Moving on to Accra, she settled Guy into college, then remained to nurse him after an automobile accident broke his neck, arm, and leg. While administering the School of Music and Drama, she starred in Bertolt Brecht's *Mother Courage* at the University of Ghana. To supplement her meager salary, she also wrote for the *Ghanaian Times* and the *African Review*, a political journal.

The African phase of Angelou's life ended with a growing sense of her American-ness. About the time of her father's death, she returned to Los Angeles, where in 1970 black spokesman Bayard Rustin sought leadership initiatives from her, including a post as Northern coordinator for the Southern Christian Leadership Conference. Two presidents—Ford and Carter—appointed her to honorary positions: the Bicentennial Commission and the National Commission on the Observance of the International Women's Year.

Subsequently, groups such as the Family Service Convention, Michigan State Celebrity Lecture series, Tennessee Humanities Council, Coalition of 100 Black Women, and Johns Hopkins University's Milton S. Eisenhower Symposium clamored for her rollicking, emotional speeches. Her humanistic topics, spiked with recitation and impromptu songs, tended toward a universal acceptance of human differences and a celebration of similarities. As she professed to one audience, "as human beings we are more alike than we are unalike. That was one of the greatest lessons I learned."

Angelou in Print. Inspired by a meeting with novelist James Baldwin, Random House editor Robert Loomis, and cartoonist Jules Feiffer and his wife, Judy, Angelou broadened her considerable store of anecdotes into autobiography, a particular strength of black writers ranging from Linda Brent and Frederick Douglass to post-slavery narratives of Eldridge Cleaver, Anne Moody, Angela Davis, Claude Brown, Malcolm X, and James Baldwin. She established a rigid working style: beginning with notes in longhand on yellow legal pads, she let the ideas flow. Then, supported by her Bible, dictionary, thesaurus, playing cards, ashtrays, snacks of cheese and bread, and bottles of sherry, she booked a downtown hotel room and sprawled across the bed, composing weekdays from six o'clock A.M. until noon, allowing no one to interfere. If the material flowed at a steady pace, she remained until early afternoon before returning to her residence. She continued for six months, going on several weeks' sabbatical, then returning to her hermitage until she had a manuscript ready for publication. By this process, in 1970, Angelou scored her first literary hit with *I Know Why the Caged Bird Sings*, an immediate bestseller and the flagship of a multi-part autobiographical armada.

In 1973 Angelou married her third husband, Paul Du Feu, an English-born carpenter and remodeler, and settled in Sonoma, California. Immersed in projects, she composed music for the movie *For the Love of Ivy*, published articles, short stories, and poems for *Harper's, Black Scholar, Mademoiselle, Redbook, Life, Playgirl, Cosmopolitan, Ebony*, and *Ladies' Home Journal*, continued writing autobiographies, produced original plays, lectured at state universities in Kansas and California, and served on the American Revolution Bicentennial Council. She earned an Emmy nomination for her cameo role as Kunta Kinte's grandmother in the 1977 television version of Alex Haley's *Roots*, adapted Sophocles's *Ajax* for the American stage, wrote for "Brewster Place," an Oprah Winfrey production, and composed songs for Roberta Flack. In 1981, after divorcing Du Feu, she received the first lifetime Reynolds Professorship of American Studies at Wake Forest University in Winston-Salem, North Carolina, where she lectures, organizes writing workshops, and continues publishing.

Again in the South. Resettlement in the South returned Angelou to home territory, where life had, at one time, seemed inequitable and discouraging to the Negro. For personal reasons, she had avoided confronting Southern bigotry for twenty-two years. As she perceived the danger, "I knew that my heart would break if ever I put my foot down on that soil, moist, still, with old hurts." To questions about her choice of roosting places, she has replied that America must embrace the people it has rejected, whose contributions might have made a considerable difference in the nation's history. Content in her twelve-room house in Old Town and with the congregation of the Mount Zion Baptist Church, she has come to grips with the reality of the days of lynching, Jim Crow, Mr. Charley, and the Ku Klux Klan. In an optimistic mood, she noted in an interview with Michele Howe of the Newark *Star-Ledger*, "It is significant and a statement of intent to give a lifetime appointment to a black and to a woman. . . . The South has changed for both blacks and whites. People are returning to their roots or moving there for the first time, and they bring new and progressive ideas with them."

Angelou's life revolves around her son, Guy, a California personnel analyst, her grandson, Colin Ashanti Murphy-Johnson, her close friend and colleague, Dolly McPherson, her long-time secretary, Mrs. Mildred Garris, and a close circle of friends and admirers, including authors Jessica Mitford, Shana Alexander, and Rosa Parks. A restless, mellow-voiced, dynamic beauty who often dresses in the bright colors and styles of Ghana, she makes herself at home in a variety of settings, both intimate and public. To interviewer Greg Hitt of the Winston-Salem *Journal*, Angelou, with her usual playful humor, remarked on a future goal: "I want to know more—not intellectually—to know more so I can be a better human being, to be an honest, courageous, funny, and loving human being. That's what I want to be—and I blow it about eighty-six times a day. My hope is to cut that to seventy."

Honors. Angelou has received a gratifying share of public acclaim. She holds honorary degrees from many academic institutions, most significantly the University of Arkansas, in the backyard of land tilled by her great-grandmother, a slave. In 1987, she accepted the North Carolina Award for Literature. Two years later, she was named one of *USA Today*'s fifty black role models. She has also been nominated for a Pulitzer Prize for poetry, a Golden Eagle film award, and an Emmy for acting, and has received fellowships from Yale University and the Rockefeller Foundation. In 1990, along with settlement worker Mother Clara Hale, she received the Candace Award, an honor extended by the National Coalition of Black Women to ten black Americans for achievement, character, and service. In 1993, she read her poem "On the Pulse of Morning" at the presidential inauguration ceremonies, and four years later she wrote the lyrics to the musical "King!" which was staged during that year's presidential inauguration to celebrate Martin Luther King Jr.'s birthday.

To all this praise, she has said, "I'm convinced that I'm a child of God. That's wonderful, exhilarating, liberating, full of promise. But the burden which goes along with that is, I'm convinced that everybody is a child of God. . . . I weep a lot. I thank God I laugh a lot, too. The main thing in one's own private world is to try to laugh as much as you cry." To an interviewer's question about her influence, she replied, "Each of us, famous or infamous, is a role model for somebody, and if we aren't, we should behave as though we are—cheerful, kind, loving, courteous. Because you can be sure someone is watching and taking deliberate and diligent notes."

INTRODUCTION TO THE BOOK

Critical Assessment.   Piqued by a dare, Angelou approached her first book as an exercise in autobiography as art, a literary achievement which, according to Random House editor Robert Loomis, is virtually impossible. Determined to transcend facts with truth, she concentrates on the Maya character's rationale and thought processes that presaged her adult character, both as woman and survivor. Disclosing her version of the black female's victimization by prejudice and powerlessness, as though creating a fictional character, she champions Maya's ability to compensate for displacement, disparagement, lack of stability, and savagely truncated self-worth. Through a tournament list of crises, young Maya moves from near-orphanhood to a rebirth of self, complete with a generous perception of worth and dignity. The circuitous pilgrimage in search of unconditional belonging ends with motherhood, ironically the failed source which precipitated Maya's soulful odyssey.

Nominated for a National Book Award in 1970 and labeled by reviewer Wanda Coleman as Angelou's "magnum opus," *I Know Why the Caged Bird Sings*, a modern classic among young adult and adult readers, has earned varied kudos. One of the most outspoken comes from the late James Baldwin, Angelou's friend and mentor: "This testimony from a black sister marks the beginning of an era in the minds and hearts and lives of all black men and women . . . Her portrait is a Biblical study of life in the midst of death." Others credit Angelou with inaugurating a new era in black consciousness and serving as a touchstone for later black female success stories, particularly the writings of Rosa Guy and Alice Walker.

Critics find much meat on the bones of Angelou's first attempt at nonfiction. Journalist Greg Hitt remarks on the recurrent **themes** of growth and self-evaluation, which she pursues with honesty and candor. Sidonie Anne Smith of *Southern Humanities Review* notes that Angelou is able to "recapture the texture of the way of life in the texture of its **idioms**, its **idiosyncratic vocabulary** and especially in its process of image-making." This unabashed joy in **metaphor** splashed with dialect and soaked in reflection comprises the book's major strength. Angelou's energetic delvings into the black community of the Depression-era South reject dolor and self-pity in favor of a full range of emotions—from wonderment at an older brother's bold, funny shenanigans to his vulnerability and dismay at a bloated corpse pulled from a pond and deposited in a jail cell—from tentative exploration of boy-girl relations to emotional release in the singing of the Negro national anthem.

In contrast, some appraisers find reason to question Angelou's notoriety as an autobiographer. In her thorough discussion of Angelou's literary style, Selwyn R. Cudjoe, in *Black Women Writers (1950–1980): A Critical Evaluation*, challenges the authenticity of the author's **point of view**, which Cudjoe suspects of distorting childhood perceptions with adult consciousness. In self-criticism, Angelou admitted to interviewer Carol E. Neubauer that maintaining a **voice** consistent with the time represented in the autobiography was difficult, but that she was encouraged enough by her early success to consider recreating some childhood incidents which, at the first writing, seemed too elusive for her skills. An unabashed fan, British reviewer Paul Bailey, sweeps away the doubts of both critic and author with frank admiration for Angelou's skillful verisimilitude: "If you want to know what it was like to live at the bottom of the heap before, during and after the American Depression, this exceptional book will tell you."

Movie Version. Angelou has said that she wanted to film *I Know Why the Caged Bird Sings* in order to "get some things on television that reflect more of the marrow of the black American life than the shallow fingernail clippings we now have." The two-hour television version, filmed in Vicksburg, Mississippi, stars Esther Rolle as Momma Henderson, Diahann Carroll and Roger Mosley as Vivian and Bailey Johnson, Ruby Dee as Grandmother Baxter, Sonny Gaines as Uncle Willie, Paul Benjamin as Mr. Freeman, John M. Driver II as Bailey Junior, and Constance Good as Maya. The production, touted in the national press as a major effort, appeared on CBS-TV as a Saturday Night Movie on April 28, 1979. According to a sprinkling of critics, the screen version, co-authored by Maya Angelou and Leonora Thuna and directed by Fielder Cook, lacked the intense yearning and lyrical introspection of the book. Stultified by television's all-too-predictable rhythms, the movie lacked the fire and spirit, warmth and sensibility that permeated her memoir and suffered from a trite ending.

The majority of critical voices, however, used words like seamless, stirring, humane, unflinchingly truthful, and intimate. In one notable review, *New Yorker* reviewer Michael J. Arlen, lauded the production for its honesty, which details "the pain of the character and the pathos of the situation." Dick Sheppard, writing for the Los Angeles *Herald Examiner*, summed up the overall effect of seeing young Maya challenge overwhelming odds as a "crescendo of power," moving viewers to a tearful consideration of the plight of a young, innocent black girl coping nobly with fearful, chaotic events.

LIST OF CHARACTERS

Marguerite "Maya" Johnson

The tall, vibrant, gifted daughter of divorced parents who lives with her paternal grandmother in the racist, unreconstructed milieu of Stamps, Arkansas. Delighting in books, which appeal to her braininess and provide escape from tedium, rigidity, and unfairness that permeate her world, Maya survives rape, but exists under an aura of guilt. Unable to bond with her flamboyant father or to mediate between her willful mother and equally willful brother, Maya copes haphazardly with familial unrest, often at the expense of peace of mind. Her coming of age, marked by doubts about the normalcy of her incipient womanhood, ends with the birth of a son, with whom she finally rediscovers a feeling of wholeness.

Bailey "Ju" Johnson, Junior

Maya's small, intense, well-read older brother, who protects and cheers her during the worst of their Stamps internment. Adept at stealing pickles from the barrel, imitating ludicrous church scenarios, and inveigling young girls into his backyard tent, Bailey remains the focal point of Maya's loyalty, the mooring to which she clings when threatened by an unstable and sometimes hostile environment. On his departure from home, he lovingly offers to care for Maya if she chooses to come along. At sea with the Merchant Marines, he remains in close contact with his sister, particularly during her pregnancy.

Momma Henderson

Former wife of Mr. Johnson, Mr. Henderson, and Mr. Murphy, Sister Annie Henderson, for twenty-five years the lone black female entrepreneur of Stamps, Arkansas, tackles daily jobs with biblical ardor and determination and never answers "questions directly put to her on any subject except religion." Eking a Depression Era living by selling fried meat pies and lemonade to local sawmill and cotton mill workers, she accepts government-issue powdered eggs and milk and canned fish in trade for store items, thereby maintaining solvency during hard times. Although poor in worldly goods and bereft of power, Annie is rich in the esteem of local people, both black and white.

Daddy Bailey Johnson

A sanguine, conceited man vain enough to send his exiled children his picture as a Christmas gift. Speaking affected but proper

English, Big Bailey, a former doorman at the Breakers Hotel in Santa Monica and later a dietician at a Naval hospital in southern California, looms larger than Maya can take in. A definite contrast to his stuttering, crippled brother and to the "peasants of Arkansas," Bailey serves temporarily as hero and rescuer after Dolores knifes Maya in the side. Failing his string of promises to Dolores, he marries Alberta.

Vivian Baxter

Affectionately known as Bibbie, Vivian, who is "Mother Dear" to her children, captivates Maya with her bold red lipstick, white teeth, Lucky Strikes, and "fresh-butter color [that] looked see-through clean." Not too prim to bash in Pat Patterson's head with a police club or shoot a two-timing business partner with her .32 , she is the most lighthearted of the grim, vindictive Baxters and covers her criminal acts with a nonchalant charm, fairness, and gaiety that bobs this side of reality, walling her off from guilt at sending her children away during crucial stages of their lives. Trained as a nurse, she earns her living "cutting poker games in gambling parlors," sometimes to the detriment of her children.

Uncle Willie

Anchored to a rubber-tipped cane and shaped like a "giant black Z" from being dropped by a babysitter when he was three years old, Uncle Willie suffers a withered left hand and distortion of muscles that pull down the left side of his face. Even more painful are the gibes of jokesters who ridicule his impairment. To facilitate counter work at the store, he leans on a special shelf. His desire for upright manhood strikes compassion in Maya.

Grandfather Baxter

Speaking his choppy West Indian dialect, Grandfather Baxter, ever in the shadow of his politically astute wife, contrasts her "throaty German accent." An invalid from the mid-1930s, he continues receiving his grandchildren at his bedside and dies a few years after Maya's return to Stamps.

Grandmother Baxter

A quadroon or octoroon, Grandmother Baxter, raised by Germans in Cairo, Illinois, was working as a nurse at Homer G. Phillips Hospital when she met Grandfather Baxter. A doughty, pragmatic precinct leader who conducts shady dealings in a thick German dialect with gracious, ladylike manners, Grandmother operates so smoothly that she glides over the matter of Mr. Freeman's murder and on to her granddaughter's health as if a gangland-style execution were business as usual. When Maya next encounters her, Grandmother Baxter, ramrod straight and adorned with pince-nez glasses, suffers chronic bronchitis and continues to smoke heavily while sharing her granddaughter's bed.

Baxter Uncles

Vivian's three older brothers—Tutti, Tom, and Ira, the oldest—notable young men with jobs in St. Louis, stand out from younger brother, Billy, by their "unrelenting meanness," which compels them to avenge Maya's rape by kicking Mr. Freeman to death. Uncle Tommy, gruff like his father, consoles Maya for not being pretty by reminding her that she is smart.

Daddy Clidell

The conservative, unassuming husband Vivian marries shortly after World War II begins. A successful but poorly educated property owner from Slaten, Texas, he is the first real father in Maya's life and teaches her to play "poker, blackjack, tonk and high, low, Jick, Jack and the Game."

Reverend Howard Thomas

Texarkana resident who presides as church elder over the district including Stamps. Hated by Maya and Bailey for being ugly, fat, and pompous, he freeloads meals from Annie. During one Sunday morning worship, his teeth fall out while he duels with Sister Monroe during her violent response to his evangelism.

Sister Monroe

An energetic, shouting churchgoer who makes up for infrequent attendance by jostling the minister and urging him to "Preach it!"

Miz Ruth, Miz Helen, Miz Eloise

Young lower-class white girls who mock Annie Henderson by imitating her posture. The tallest one does a handstand in the dust, revealing her bare backside as an extra dollop of disrespect.

Mrs. Bertha Flowers

A cool, thin, black-skinned Stamps matron who, with her voile dresses, flowered hats, and white gloves, embodies a refined, ladylike grace that is the **antithesis** of local squalor and misery. As baker of tea cookies, reader of Dickens, and representative of what Momma calls "settled people," Mrs. Flowers is an appropriate antidote to Maya's poignant self-loathing.

Viola Cullinan

Maya's white acquisitive and tradition-bound employer and the barren wife of Mr. Cullinan, who fathered the Coleman girls, two attractive daughters of a Stamps black woman. Perceiving herself as Virginia-born elite, Mrs. Cullinan precipitates an early burst of rebellion in Maya by renaming her Mary, thereby denying her personhood. Shrieking for her mother's forgiveness, Mrs. Cullinan offers comic relief by wallowing among the fragments of her ruined dinnerware.

Louise Kendricks

Louise, the daughter of a domestic worker, is a lonely girl and fellow ten year old who shares Maya's dreamy romanticism as well as the Tut language, a secret child's language. Loss of Louise's friendship is Maya's sole regret in departing from Stamps.

Tommy Valdon

Maya's first male admirer, an eighth-grader who, without knowledge of her past, reawakens shreds of rape trauma.

Joyce

A sexually precocious fourteen year old who seduces ten-year-old Bailey, instigating his petty thievery of sardines, Polish sausage, cheese, and canned salmon from the store, then runs away to Dallas, Texas, to marry a railroad porter, one of a group of Elks that she met in Momma's Store.

George Taylor

A recent widower after forty years of marriage to wife Florida. Mr. Taylor, owlish, bald, wizened, and pathetic, visits Annie Henderson's house at suppertime to tell about a request for children from his wife's ghost.

Mr. Edward Donleavy

A condescending white politician from Texarkana who patronizes Maya's graduating class by stereotyping their heroes as athletes and limiting their horizons to mundane trades, then exits the stage to attend to more important matters in the white world.

Henry Reed

Valedictorian of the 1940 graduating class of Lafayette County Training School. Raised by his grandmother and trained by his teachers in elocution, he earns Maya's qualified regard for reciting "To Be or Not To Be" from Shakespeare's *Hamlet*, then lifts the general mood by leading his class in an impromptu singing of the Negro national anthem, James Weldon Johnson's "Lift Ev'ry Voice and Sing."

Mr. Freeman

A large, flabby Southerner who unashamedly worships Vivian, his paramour, following her out of the room with adoring eyes. A foreman for the Southern Pacific Railroad, Mr. Freeman spends his life waiting for Vivian's return. Faceless, sinister, and smelling of coal dust and grease, he sexually abuses eight-year-old Maya, then rapes her. After stopping by her bed to repeat his threat against her brother if she reveals his crimes, Mr. Freeman departs from Vivian's house. His murder, although grisly, seems well deserved.

Miss Kirwin

Maya's civics and current events teacher at George Washington High School in San Francisco. A twenty-year veteran with memorable stature and "battleship-gray hair," she impresses Maya by respecting teenagers enough to refer to them as "ladies and gentlemen."

Red Leg

Along with Just Black, Stonewall Jimmy, Cool Clyde, and Tight Coat, Red Leg, a quick-witted underworld friend of Daddy Clidell, entertains Maya with a long-winded story of how he conned a Tulsa cracker.

Dolores Stockland

Bailey Johnson's prim, pretentious small-framed girl friend, who interrupts her meticulous sewing of kitchen curtains to vent her temper and jealousy on Maya by stabbing her in the side.

Bootsie

A tall boy who serves as spokesman for the rules of the junkyard commune where Maya lives. He maintains group finances by keeping everyone's earnings and doling them out equitably.

Lee Arthur

The only member of the junkyard commune who lives at home. Lee welcomes the gang to his house on Friday evenings for baths.

CRITICAL COMMENTARIES

INTRODUCTION

Rising out of childhood's bitter memories of a too-long cut-down lavender Easter dress made from "a white woman's once-was-purple throwaway," Marguerite "Maya" Johnson, the **central intelligence**, or key voice, well into adulthood, recalls in a **flashback** her fantasy of being suddenly transformed into a white girl and her intense need to be excused from church services. Unable to contain her urine on the church porch, she wets her clothes; then, sure that she will be punished for misbehavior, laughingly embraces her sense of freedom.

The opening lines introduce a crucial **theme**—the Maya character's movie-star dream of being so blond-haired and blue-eyed that she amazes onlookers. The scenario, heavily laced with rhythm, dialect, alliteration, and exacting imagery, reveals two of the author's strengths—her natural gift for language and her insistence on an upbeat, gentle self-deprecation, easily flowing from the humor sparked by **incongruity** and **wit.** Against the fairy godmother fantasy, she reveals that in reality she is a "too-big Negro girl, with nappy black hair, broad feet and a space between her teeth that would hold a number-two pencil." As she internalizes her blackness, she equates it with ugliness, a self-image that clouds her childhood. In the last paragraph of her surrealistic exit from church, Angelou utilizes **sensory impressions** to dramatize her need to urinate, describing the urge as a "green persimmon, or it could have been a lemon, [which] caught me between the legs and squeezed." The forward rolling pitch that hurtles the small girl down the aisle presages the underlying **rhythms** that move her through the rest of the narrative against a tide of setbacks and disappointments that scarcely daunt her determined passage.

(Here and in the following sections, difficult words, phrases, and colloquialisms are translated for you, as are these below.)

- **Colored Methodist Episcopal Church** an African-American offshoot of the Southern Methodist Church, which withdrew from the parent church in 1870 as a separate entity devoted to the evangelizing of Africa's non-Christians. In May 1954, members voted to rename it the Christian Methodist Episcopal Church.

CHAPTERS 1–3

After the divorce of their parents, three-year-old Maya and her brother, Bailey, Jr., a year her senior, tagged like freight, arrive at the Wm. Johnson General Merchandise Store, Momma Henderson's grocery and feed store in Stamps, Arkansas. Daily, field workers pass through the store to buy supplies, impressing the Maya character, or the speaker, with the anguish of their ill-paid labors. From the outset, the author demonstrates a **humanistic** sympathy for the downtrodden Southern black. Her skilled theatrical eye differentiates black misery as seen by soft early morning glow and later, by the harsher afternoon sun, which spotlights the field laborer's hand-to-mouth struggle against low wages, long hours, and soul-wearying drudgery. As a blessing on this near-slave level of subsistence, the author discloses Momma's simple pre-dawn prayer, a stoic **litany** which thanks God for one more day of life.

At age five, Maya, later singled out by Momma for her tender heart, is astute enough to realize that Uncle Willie's contorted body lessens his manhood. He appeases psychic pain by concealing his affliction from two strangers from Little Rock. As an adult, Angelou probes a greater denigration by conjuring up the "cement faces and eyes" of Klansmen "covered with graves' dust and age without beauty of learning," which **symbolize** the hatred of the most rabid of Arkansas racists. Uncle Willie, too lame to ward off the feared night riders, moans his helplessness from layers of potatoes and onions, which conceal his form in the vegetable bin "like a casserole."

- **c/o**   a postal abbreviation for "in care of."

- **The Brazos**   a Texas river, flowing past Waco to Freeport on the Gulf of Mexico through stereotypical cowboy country.

- **juice harp (Jew's harp)**   a metal or bamboo percussion instrument common to Europe and Asia since ancient times and originally named a jaw harp. Holding the harp between the teeth, the player vibrates the central stem with strums of the finger while changing positions of the mouth, tongue, and jaw to alter the resulting twangy tones.

- **fo' bits and six bits**   fifty cents and seventy-five cents.

- **paranoia**   an abnormal mental state which often causes the sufferer to feel persecuted.

- **cotton bolls**   the hard, prickly, taloned, fibrous pod which encases a growing fluff of cotton and thwarts the picker's efforts.

- **Butler; Henley**   Samuel Butler (1835–1902), author of *Erewhon* and *The Way of All Flesh*, and William Ernest Henley (1849–1903), author of the poem "Invictus," which students often memorize for its bold espousal of self-determination and individualism.

- **abacuses**   counting frames composed of color-coded beads that are slid along rods or wires for quick hand calculation; still popular in Japan and other Eastern countries.

CHAPTERS 4–5

As speaker, Maya describes the rigidly segregated social **milieu** of Stamps, with its alien "whitefolksville" and despicable, twangy-voiced "powhitetrash." She delineates her relationship with relatives near and distant, but never strays far from her brother, Bailey, the center and mainstay of her scattered family. She loves him for being "small, graceful and smooth," executing petty larcenies from the pickle barrel without getting caught, and, most important, accepting her in spite of her lack of physical beauty. With unabashed **hyperbole**, she dubs him "my Kingdom Come."

In Chapter 5, the unpalatable memory of Momma's humiliation by coarse, impudent white girls forces out a greater exaggeration: "The world had taken a deep breath and was having doubts about continuing to revolve." The sharp, stabbing memory of seeing her godly, longsuffering grandmother shamed by so slatternly a trio as "Miz Ruth," "Miz Helen," and "Miz Eloise" elevates Momma, whose real beauty lies in her resigned chorus of "Glory, glory, hallelujah, when I lay my burden down." With the beneficence of childhood, Maya shapes concentric hearts in the dust and pierces them with a love arrow, emblematic of her bond with the strongest female figure in her life.

- **Texarkana**   twin cities on the border of Texas and Arkansas.

- **clabbered milk**   curdled, or soured milk.

- **cat-o'-nine-tails**   a whip fashioned from loose strands which end in knots that leave clawlike marks on a victim's body.

- **pooched out**   protruded.

CHAPTERS 6–7

Masterfully melding her **tone** from raucous naughty fun into the grim and everpresent menace of white violence against the imagined threat from Negro sexuality, the author foreshadows Maya's childhood ambivalence toward men. Intuitively, she eludes the embrace of Reverend Howard Thomas, a persistent mooch at the Henderson table, but revels in Bailey's eavesdropping on the minutiae of local gossip about sexual misconduct that the minister shares with Momma. The high quality of **imagery** captures the color and flavor of ample Sunday morning breakfasts, particularly the menu: crunchy fried perch, tomato slices drenched in ham drippings, and cathead biscuits which, if allowed to cool during the minister's overlong table blessings, "tended to a gooeyness, not unlike a wad of tired gum."

Angelou's skill at recreating the fervor of Southern black funda-mentalism retreats from dogma to the unremitting humor of Sister Monroe's ebullient **counterpoint** against the elder's sermon. The duet, an unrehearsed, madcap Laurel-and-Hardy act which leaves churchgoers "hung loose like stockings on a washline," convulses the children, who, riveted to the front-row mourners' bench in sight of Momma and Uncle Willie, explode in uncontrollable laughter. Amid the furor of a worship service gone awry, the young Maya reveals a significant emotional defense, the ability to "not see or hear if [she] chose not to do so," a protective armor which **foreshadows** her later ego defense mechanism against the terror and guilt of rape. In con-trast to her self-induced limbo of emotions, by the end of the scene, she breaches the slim divider that separates laughter and tears. She notes, "Laughter so easily turns to hysteria for imaginative children. I felt for weeks after that I had been very, very sick . . ."

- **elder**   minister in charge of district church management.

- **Gladstone**   hand luggage composed of cloth or leather sides attached to a rigid frame.

- **Suffer little children to come unto me, for such is the Kingdom of Heaven.**   as found in Matthew 19:14, Mark 10:14, and Luke 18:16, a vari-ation of Jesus' words to his disciples, who rejected children who accompa-nied their parents to see and hear Jesus.

- **When I was a child I spake as a child, I thought as a child, but when I became a man, I put away childish things.**   verse eleven from I Corin-thians 13, one of the most quoted chapters in the New Testament Bible, which deals with charity.

- **God is not mocked.**   a portion of verse seven from Paul's letter to the Galatians, in which he warns that "whatsoever a man soweth, that shall he also reap."

- **cater-cornered**   diagonally.

- **mourners' bench**   a front row reserved for people troubled about illness or personal problems. Mourners sat before others who might see their suf-fering and join in their prayers.

- **I came to Jesus, as I was, worried, wound, and sad, I found in Him a resting place and He has made me glad.**   an approximation of the third and fourth lines of verse one of "I Heard the Voice of Jesus Say," an evange-listic hymn written by John B. Dykes in 1868 to a tune by Horatius Bonar.

- **the eighteenth chapter of the Gospel according to St. Luke** a crucial chapter in the Christian gospel which defines justice, describes the appropriate way to pray and the contrition required of a suppliant of God, predicts the fulfillment of Old Testament prophecies, and concludes with an act of healing.

- **Mount Nebo** the elevation from which Moses observed the Promised Land, as described in Deuteronomy 34:1-4.

- **Naked I came into the world, and naked I shall go out.** an approximation of Job 1:21, which is echoed in Ecclesiastes 5:15.

- **George Raft** popular character actor of the 1930s and 40s who frequently played smooth, menacing underworld figures in gangster movies.

- **sobriquet** nickname, or code name.

- **chifforobe** a combination chest of drawers and wardrobe.

CHAPTERS 8–9

Opening with Angelou's frequently quoted **diatribe**, or denunciation, against Southern racism, Chapter 8 maintains the funny/sad **tension** of earlier scenes by depicting the behind-the-times Negroes of Stamps as unaware of the Depression. Reduced to even harder times, country people are too poor to raise hogs because they have no slops to feed them, but the wily Annie Henderson devises a trade agreement to keep herself in business. At this all-time low in the family economy, when Maya and Bailey are reduced to daily portions of powdered milk and eggs, their parents reconnect with their lives, first with Christmas presents, which torture Maya and Bailey with fears that they have precipitated their own banishment, then with a surprise visit from Daddy Bailey. Angelou recalls that "my seven-year-old world humpty-dumptied, never to be put back together again." In her distress over the white doll and tea set, Maya, lost in childhood's illogic, fails to consider that toys designed specifically for black children were not available in the 1930s.

As Momma quietly sews for Maya's departure, the bond between them remains nonverbal, but Angelou notes that "a deep-brooding love hung over everything [Momma] touched." Sunk in self-made emotional packing, Maya shuts out the impending loss of brother Bailey as the center of her life and contemplates reuniting with her mother. Returning to her earlier flair for **hyperbole** from nature,

Maya describes Vivian as a "hurricane in its perfect power. Or the climbing, falling colors of a rainbow." The immediate shift of family alliances leaves Maya on the outside after her father departs and her beloved Bailey falls under the spell of "Mother Dear." As Angelou sums up her alienation in characteristic **vernacular**: "They both had physical beauty and personality, so I figured it figured."

- **cat's face** a wrinkled patch which is inadvertently ironed into freshly laundered clothes or linens.

- **play pretties** toys.

- **God is love.** John 4:8.

- **Pig Latin** a child's private jargon of the 1930s created by placing the initial consonant plus *ay* at the end of the word, as in *ooday* for *do*.

- **indlay ergbay ildrenchay** literally, lindberg children—that is, victims of kidnapping, like Charles Lindbergh, Jr., who was later found murdered.

CHAPTERS 10–11

A shift in locale alters the **tempo** of *I Know Why the Caged Bird Sings*. From the microcosm of Stamps to that of Caroline Street in St. Louis, Maya and Bailey travel light-years away from the simplistic morality and Bible-decreed fundamentalism of Grandmother Annie Henderson to the seamy, potentially violent underworld precinct superintended by Grandmother Baxter. Given their firm Southern upbringing and academic promise, Maya and Bailey cope well with school. At home, they continue to marvel at their sybaritic mother, the kind of woman Angelou epitomizes in *Now Sheba Sings the Song* as "Lip smacking, finger snapping, toe tapping/ Shoulder bouncing, hip throwing, breast thrusting, eye flashing, /Love of good and God and Life." A foil to her inarticulate, cunning three older brothers, Vivian moves Maya and Bailey to the house she shares with her paramour, Mr. Freeman, to make a weak attempt at motherhood.

Perpetually insecure, Maya, who suffers from nightmares and at times longs to be a boy, perceives herself as a temporary guest among her Baxter relatives. **Ironically**, retreat to her mother's bed places her in immediate jeopardy—alongside the lustful child ravisher who eventually annihilates her innocence. In recounting the violation,

Maya resorts to **euphemisms** that she learned in Stamps: "thing" for "penis" and "pocketbook" for "vagina." The supporting **images**— helpless piglets awaiting slaughter, the "inside of a freshly killed chicken," and even fears that Mr. Freeman will die from sexual ecstasy—replicate the silent death that later reduces Maya to a near zombie-like state.

Unaccustomed to fatherly attentions, the naive Maya, held fast in strong arms, fantasizes that Mr. Freeman is her real parent. In a bitter **anticlimax**, her abuser rolls over, "leaving [her] in a wet place" and blaming her for urinating on the bed. Doleful because she faces yet another rejection, she fears that he will never cuddle her again. From the clarity of adult perspective, Angelou concludes: "It was the same old quandary. I had always lived it. There was an army of adults, whose motives and movements I just couldn't understand and who made no effort to understand mine."

- **numbers runners**   petty street criminals who collect money from people betting on a lucky number.

- **pince-nez**   eyeglasses which have no temple pieces and which rely on a spring to secure them to the bridge of the nose.

- **had pull with**   influenced.

- **German *Brot***   dark, round glazed loaves of rye or wheat bread.

- **Toussaint L'Ouverture**   François-Dominique Toussaint-L'Ouverture (1743–1803), military leader and liberator of Haiti.

- **siditty**   pretentious.

- **Alley Oop**   the dinosaur-riding cave man and beau of Ooola, both characters in V. T. Hamlin's popular cartoon strip, which originated in 1933.

- **The Shadow**   a popular radio program premiering on the CBS "Detective Story" in August 1930, which grew from Walter Gibson's serialized novels in *Street and Smith* Magazine. The character was originally played by Jack LaCurto; in 1937 Orson Welles assumed the role.

- **Horatio Alger**   graduate of Harvard Divinity School, Alger (1832–99) wrote 130 books in three series—Ragged Dick, Luck and Pluck, and Tattered Tom—about determined boys who work their way up from poverty and obscurity to fame and riches. Altogether, the Horatio Alger series sold twenty million copies.

- **Tiny Tim**   beloved crippled son of Bob Cratchit in Charles Dickens' classic novel *A Christmas Carol*, published in serial form in 1843.

- **Katzenjammer Kids**   cartoon characters in a New York *Journal* strip drawn by Rudolph Dirks. A hybrid version of *Max and Moritz*, a German cartoon, the strip was first printed in 1897.

CHAPTERS 12–13

The central violent **episode** in Maya's young life occurs significantly on a day following one of her mother's unheralded overnight absences. The **atmosphere**, a bizarre mix of menace and fantasies of comic strip rescuers, recedes into white after Maya faints from pain. Harsh, unpleasant physical sensations blend with pretense as she stoically conceals her hurt to save Bailey from certain death at the hands of the tormenter who transgresses her little girl trust. In a rapid, **surrealistic** flow of events, Maya, comforted by her dutiful navy blue coat with brass buttons, takes the stand and conceals from the court her first two sexual encounters with Mr. Freeman. Consumed by guilt, she screams, "Ole, mean, dirty thing, you. Dirty old thing" and is removed from the stand to Vivian's embrace. Appropriately, Mr. Freeman's ignominious demise behind the slaughterhouse ends with Grandmother Baxter's injunction against "that evil man's name." Fearful of spreading a curse on her loved ones, Maya stops talking to anyone but Bailey.

- **the Phantom**   Ray Moore's cartoon, which first appeared in daily newspapers in February 17, 1936, advanced to comic books, and was made into a movie serial in 1943 and a TV animation in 1986.

- **the Green Hornet**   a popular radio show which originated on WXYZ Detroit on January 31, 1936, and continued until December 5, 1952. The Hornet, the great nephew of the Lone Ranger, was created by George W. Trendle and written by Fran Striker, who also wrote episodes of *The Lone Ranger.*

- **Sloan's Liniment**   an astringent balm used to treat strains and sprains.

- *The Rover Boys*   a twenty-volume young adult series written by Edward Stratemeyer under the pseudonym Arthur M. Winfield. Stratemeyer also wrote the Tom Swift, Bobbsey Twins, Nancy Drew, and Hardy Boys series, a total of over eight hundred books.

- **harlot in the Bible**   John 8:3–11.

- **recording angel**   Revelation 10:1–11.

CHAPTERS 14–15

Mentally "stepping over the border lines of the map" like a game of emotional hopscotch, Maya, returned by train without explanation to the "Southern bitter wormwood" of Stamps, fears that she will drop off the edge of the earth. Sensitive to scrutiny since her brutal St. Louis experience, she rejects Uncle Willie's pity as the sympathy of a cripple. Unmoored from past security, she allies herself spiritually and academically with Mrs. Bertha Flowers, a mannerly, gossamer presence "sweet-milk fresh," whose "lessons in living" introduce her to the refined art of recitation. The boost in self-esteem is the lifeline that Maya needs to carry her through post-rape trauma. Inexplicably, Momma Henderson, a perpetual enforcer eager to carry out her interpretation of scriptural decree, shatters Maya's upbeat mood by forcing her to her knees and whipping her for (unknowingly) slighting God. The senseless violence to Maya's spirit, although not on a par with Mr. Freeman's rupture of her tender body, epitomizes the children's complete powerlessness at the whims of adults.

- **double entendres**   expressions which carry two possible interpretations, one of which is often coarse or obscene.

- **moors**   grassy wastelands, often the misty, mysterious settings in Gothic fiction.

- **scones and crumpets**   biscuits and cakes usually served with tea.

- **morocco-bound**   covered in fine leather.

- **two last names divided by a hyphen**   the European custom of naming a child both the father's and mother's surnames.

- **French seams**   a method of doubly securing two pieces of cloth by folding over the edges of a seam and sewing a second time.

- **Pride is a sin . . . it goeth before a fall**   a paraphrase of Proverbs 16:18.

- **brother would turn against brother**   an approximation of Mark 13:12.

- **a gnashing of teeth**   a frequent New Testament image, found in Matthew 8:12, 13:42, 22:13, 24:51, 25:30, and Luke 13:28.

CHAPTER 16

From the gentle lessons of Mrs. Flowers, Maya, like a dusky imitation of a white debutante, advances to the kitchen of Mrs. Viola Cullinan, where she learns the mysteries of china and silver. Pointedly, amid the proper and prestigious array of dishes and glassware, the drinking vessels of Miss Glory and Maya sit "on a separate shelf from the others," mute testimony to the racism that lurks as a silent third party between kitchen servant and lady of the house. Ironically, Maya wastes tender sympathies on her barren employer, who appears unaware of the handsome offspring of the faceless Mr. Cullinan and his Negro mistress. The explosive comedy of "Mary's" departure from her white mistress's service is a welcome **comic relief** from the tension of earlier chapters.

The obvious difference in **point of view** between Maya and Miss Glory presages the coming civil rights struggle, when black workers rebelled against Uncle Tom stereotypes and refused to act the part of the compliant, well-schooled darky. In the line of fire when Mrs. Cullinan launches a poorly aimed salvo of jagged crockery pieces, Miss Glory, suitably punished for her old-fashioned subservience, catches a chunk over the ear. In a more pronounced example of **poetic justice**, as though assaulting her predecessors for their weak-kneed toadying, the speaker describes young Maya as walking out on the melee and leaving the door open to broadcast the plaintive dismay of her employer.

- **married beneath her**   married below her social station.

- **Cheshire cat's smile**   continuing the image from *Alice in Wonderland*, a reference to the cat which disembodies itself, leaving only its smile behind.

CHAPTER 17

Enriched by warm, fuzzy memories of Saturdays, worm gardens, a chinaberry tree, shining shoes with a biscuit, and ten cents' allowance, Chapter 17 moves optimistically away from Maya's earlier sufferings. Then, without warning, the plot yo-yos back to the dark side when Bailey stays late at a movie to see a white actress—Kay Francis, whom Bailey describes as being the image of "Mother Dear." His unexplained absence leaves the family on the raw rim of anxiety. Momma's overreaction to his tardiness stems from the fear of the "hanging noose," the capricious racist violence that traditionally snatches away "sons, grandsons and nephews."

Willing to undergo humiliation and punishment to retain his secret, weeks later, Bailey shares the entrancing screen star with Maya when the next Kay Francis movie comes to Stamps. Angelou uses the opportunity to skewer movieland's black caricatures and the variations in response from white cinema-goers and their black counterparts, relegated to the colored balcony. Ending the episode with an unexpected burst of rebellion from Bailey, she divulges that a year later, Bailey hops a train and exits her life in a brief attempt to locate his "Mother Dear." Her droll side note pictures him stranded in Baton Rouge, nowhere near his beloved parent.

- **mumbledypeg**   a game requiring participants to flip a knife so that the blade sticks in the ground, often between the toes of the player.

- **tithe**   a percentage of income (usually ten percent) donated regularly to the church in obedience to the specific command of Malachi 3:10: "Bring ye all the tithes into the storehouse that there might be meat in mine house."

- **Rye-al-toh**   A standard name for movie theaters is Rialto, taken from a highly ornate bridge over the Grand Canal in Venice, Italy.

- **Bluebeards**   killers like the protagonist of Charles Perrault's French folktales, written in 1697.

- **Rippers**   slashers of women, like the self-named Jack the Ripper, the unidentified mangler of seven London prostitutes from August 7 to November 10, 1888.

CHAPTERS 18–19

Returning to the **themes** of Chapters 1 and 6, Angelou cross-examines her own attitudes toward Southern black behavior, particularly the penchant for religiosity. Puzzled by the willingness of bone-weary field hands to settle for leftover food so that they will have time to attend late night revival meetings, she attributes their choice to masochism and notes, ". . . not only was it our fate to live the poorest, roughest life but that we liked it like that." Her portrait of the "transitory setting" of tent evangelism is a faithful rendering of a

Southern tradition: the impermanence of folding chairs, two by fours holding up makeshift strings of lights, and canvas walls undulating with the breeze.

Angelou, ever watchful for a bit of **tongue-in-cheek** humor, milks the scene for its **undercurrent** of pubescent coming of age rites and small town snobbery, where the high-toned denizens of Mount Zion Baptist Church contrast with the more cerebral African Methodist Episcopal and their counterparts in the African Methodist Episcopal Zion, and the proletarian Christian Methodist Episcopal church. On the outskirts of Christian respectability lurk the fervid Holy Rollers, who spare no exertions as they "make a joyful noise." She swiftly **segues** into the soulful give-and-take of minister with congregation, the singing of a dolorous hymn, scripture readings, and a lengthy harangue encouraging charity. To Stamps's poorest, whom Angelou dubs "society's pariahs" and "America's historic bowers and scrapers," the minister's welcome prophecy indicates that uncharitable whites will "get their comeuppance," a sweet revenge for a protracted history of injustice. The **catharsis** wrought by spiritual surrender spreads like contagion, concluding in a reception for repentent sinners and a maudlin **coda** of mothers crooning a reminder that they have limited time to see their children safely locked into the Christian fold. Smug and self-righteous in their salvation, the elect walk home amid bluesy tunes from a local roadhouse, which provides a cheery alternative to tent revival **escapism**.

In Chapter 19, still probing the theme of deliverance, Angelou shifts the setting from the cool night air to the packed intensity of bodies crouched over the store radio to hear a broadcast of a crucial prize fight. Local blacks, **identifying** so intensely with Joe Louis that they become one with him through ups and downs of the bout, interpret his trials in the same category with lynchings, beatings, and pursuit by hounds. The scene not only depicts the culture of the radio era, but also explains and justifies African-American hero worship of black athletes.

- **Raise up a child in the way he should go and he will not depart from it** a paraphrase of Proverbs 22:6.

- **Make a joyful noise unto the Lord, and be exceedingly glad** an amalgam of Psalm 100:1 with Matthew 5:12.

- **"Precious Lord, Take My Hand"**   hymn which is a standard feature of fundamentalist revival services because of its crooning, mournful melody, melodramatic images, and gentle harmonies.

- **C.M.E. Church**   Colored Methodist Episcopal Church.

- **Matthew, twenty-fifth chapter, thirtieth verse through the forty-sixth**   one of Jesus' sermons in which he reminds the faithful that he will return from a heavenly throne to question people about their charity toward "the least of these"—that is, the hungry, thirsty, alienated, naked, and imprisoned.

- **First Corinthians**   a loose rendering of I Corinthians 13:1, 3, which encourages charity.

- **in that great Gettin' Up Morning**   a Negro spiritual that describes resurrection in idiomatic terms.

- **separate the sheep (them) from the goats (the whitefolks)**   a reference to an image in Matthew 25:32 which pictures the separation of the saved from the unsaved as the action of a shepherd dividing sheep from goats, which are known to be quarrelsome with more peaceable animals.

- **now abideth faith, hope and charity, these three; but the greatest of these is charity**   I Corinthians 13:13, the conclusion of Paul's essay on charity.

- **John Brown**   American abolitionist who was hanged in 1859 for leading a raid on the federal arsenal at Harper's Ferry, Virginia.

- **He who can hear, let him hear**   an altered version of Ezekiel 3:27.

- **before one word of this changes, heaven and earth shall fall away**   a paraphrase of Jesus' promise in Matthew 5:18.

- **barrelhouse blues**   a pulsing, unmelodious jazz beat.

- **How long, oh God? How long?**   a plea often heard in spirituals, possibly having its roots in Psalms 13:1 and Isaiah 6:11. George Bernard Shaw ends his drama *Saint Joan* with Joan asking, "How long, O Lord, how long?"

- **cracker**   a disparaging, derogatory slang term for a white, bigoted, violent Southerner.

- **string-along songs about razor blades**   Radio prize-fight broadcasts were sponsored by Gillette.

- **Louis**   world heavyweight champion from 1937–49, Joe Louis (1914–81), nicknamed the "Brown Bomber," racked up a record of sixty-eight victories in seventy-one fights.

- **master's voice**   part of a slogan affixed to RCA Victor radios and phonographs along with a picture of a dog listening to sounds coming from the horn of a victrola.

- **Carnera**   Primo Carnera, whom Joe Louis defeated on June 25, 1935.

CHAPTERS 20–23

In a respite from the more serious themes of the autobiography, Angelou's reminiscences about early adolescence, when forging friendships, receiving love notes, exchanging valentines, sizing up a male admirer, and completing eighth grade take precedence over her concern for equality and self-determination for the black race. A **cameo** of Americana at the end of the 1930s, Angelou's picture of women frying fish and arranging barbecued chickens and spareribs, baked ham, and homemade pickles and cakes on picnic tables, children playing ring games, Bailey and Maya lugging watermelons into the Coca-Cola box and filling an iron washpot with ice, and gospel singers warming up for a performance supplies the African-American counterpart of a Norman Rockwell print or an oil painting of a neighborhood outing by Grandma Moses. Freed from the devastating emotional turmoil of earlier chapters, Maya, while guarding the gnawing secret of rape by Mr. Freeman, finds time to gaze at clouds and share intimate girl talk with her contemporary, Louise Kendricks.

No less evocative of Southern culture of the early 1940s, Maya's eighth-grade graduation from the no-frills Lafayette County Training School, recounted in nostalgic, bittersweet glimpses, highlights a processional through "a few shady tall persimmon trees," gifts of money, handkerchiefs, a book of Edgar Allan Poe's works, a new dress, and a Mickey Mouse watch from friends and relatives, a breakfast worthy of Sunday morning, and, for a few fellow students, ready-made outfits from Sears and Roebuck or Montgomery Ward or makeovers of hand-me-downs for those who cannot afford new clothes. The second singing of the Negro national anthem, a traditional rallying song since its publication in 1900, negates the denigrating oration of the supercilious Mr. Edward Donleavy and revives Maya from a temporary letdown. For the first time, she internalizes the familiar words and realizes that "Black known and unknown poets" (including "preachers, musicians and blues singers") have had a significant role in uplifting African-Americans.

- **Acka Backa, Sody Cracka . . .**   a typical jump rope rhyme, similar to "Rich man, poor man" and Angelou's mimetic poem "Harlem Hopscotch."

- **Elks**   a men's benevolent, ritualist, and fraternal order which began in 1868.

- **Eastern Star**   a fraternal order, founded in 1876, composed of Master Masons and female relatives and dedicated to service, fellowship, and civic responsibilities.

- **Masons**   a men's charitable service organization, founded in 1797.

- **Knights of Columbus**   a fraternal organization, founded in 1882 and limited to Catholic males.

- **Daughters of Pythias**   a women's auxiliary of the Knights of Pythias, founded in 1864 as a charitable and fraternal order.

- **chow-chow**   a piquant or hot pickled relish made from a variety of garden vegetables, particularly cucumber, cabbage, carrot, pepper, and onion, and served with blander foods, such as pinto, lima, or navy beans.

- **viewing gauze**   a layer of opaque cloth placed over the face of a corpse before public viewing, often to conceal deterioration or deep wounds.

- **Captain Marvel**   a comic book character created by Carl Burgos and Bill Everett and first appearing in print in November 1939.

- **teenincy**   Southern dialect for very small.

- **The Lord giveth and the Lord taketh away . . . Blessed be the name of the Lord**   Job 1:21, a stoic verse often cited at funerals and graveside rites.

- **my brother was far away on a raft on the Mississippi**   that is, Bailey was immersed in Mark Twain's *The Adventures of Huckleberry Finn*.

- **hants**   haunts, or ghosts.

- **juju**   magic resulting from use of a charm or amulet.

- **jacks**   a coordination game requiring the player to bounce a ball and toss and pick up a series of six-pointed metal game pieces.

- **Jordan**   a river in Palestine where John the Baptist baptized Jesus. In Christian hymnology, "crossing the Jordan" symbolizes the soul's passage into heaven.

- **thou art my good and faithful servant with whom I am well pleased**   an approximation of Jesus' words in the parable of the talents, Matthew 25:21.

- **I hungered . . .**   a random summary of Matthew 25: 35–40.

I Know Why the Caged Bird Sings
Genealogy & Pertinent Maps

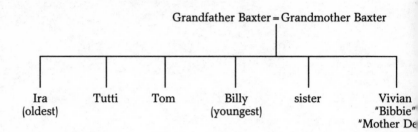

Grandfather Baxter = Grandmother Baxter

Ira	Tutti	Tom	Billy	sister	Vivian
(oldest)			(youngest)		"Bibbie"
					"Mother De

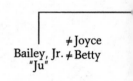

Bailey, Jr. ≠ Joyce
"Ju" ≠ Betty

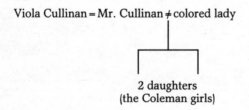

Viola Cullinan = Mr. Cullinan ≠ colored lady

2 daughters
(the Coleman girls)

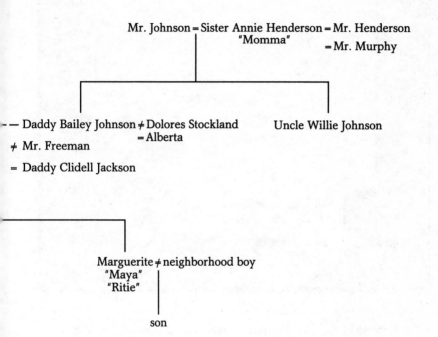

	divorced
=	married
≠	lovers

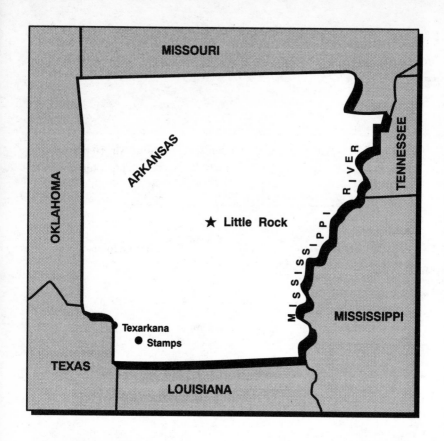

Born in St. Louis, Missouri, Maya spends most of her childhood in **Stamps, Arkansas**, where she is raised by her grandmother, Momma Annie Johnson. Shortly after her eighth grade graduation, Maya suffers an excruciating toothache and after the local white dentist refuses to treat her, she is taken by Momma to a black dentist in **Texarkana.**

Later, Maya and her brother, Bailey, Jr., move to California, living about six months in **Los Angeles**, then moving north to **Oakland**, where they live with their mother, Vivian, and finally they settle in **San Francisco**, after Vivian marries Daddy Clidell.

During a visit to her father's trailer in an unnamed city in southern California, Daddy Bailey takes Maya to **Ensenada, Mexico**; when she discovers that he is too drunk to drive home, Maya has to steer the car down fifty miles of steep, winding roads to **Calexico, California.**

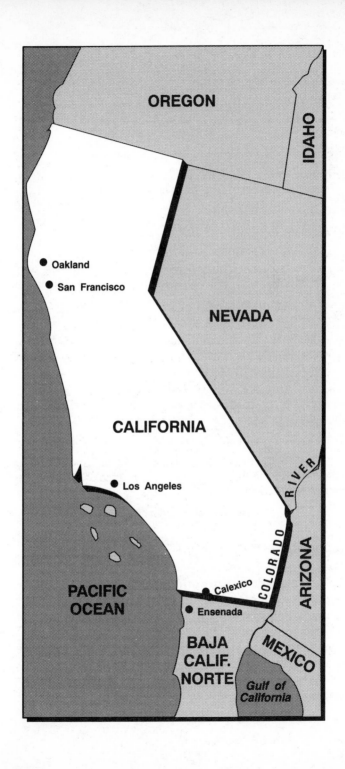

- **Ashes to ashes and dust to dust**   from the burial service in the Book of Common Prayer.

- **cyclopean eye**   In Greek mythology, the cyclopes were a race of one-eyed giants.

- **Peace, be still**   Jesus' command to the sea, Mark 5:39.

- **Montgomery Ward**   a department store chain that offered mail order service from large catalogues that were sent to the public.

- **piqué**   a sturdy ribbed fabric.

- **Let your light so shine . . .**   part of Jesus' Sermon on the Mount, Matthew 5:16.

- **backsliders**   a common fundamentalist pejorative for people who were once Christian, but who gradually return to faithlessness or immorality.

- **Mickey Mouse**   Walt Disney's star of animated cartoons, who debuted in 1928.

- **Fisk**   a university founded in Nashville, Tennessee, in 1866 and famous for such noteworthy graduates as writer W. E. B. Du Bois and poet Nikki Giovanni.

- **Owens**   Jesse Owens, son of an Alabama sharecropper, triumphed in track and field at the 1936 Olympic games in Berlin against a background of Nazi racism, which favored the blue-eyed blonds of the Aryan race.

- **Gabriel Prosser**   leader of a slave revolt in 1800 in Richmond, Virginia.

- **Nat Turner**   leader of a slave revolt on August 21, 1831, which ended with the deaths of sixty white victims and the execution of Turner and sixteen other insurrectionists.

- **Amazon**   one of a race of female warriors mentioned in Homer's *Iliad*.

CHAPTERS 24–25

The double-ended **tragicomic scenario** involving Maya's aching tooth epitomizes Angelou's ability to interweave serious theme with gentle humor. Against the cruelty and lack of professionalism of a dentist (ironically named Dr. Lincoln) who would vilify a suffering child and refuse her medical attention because of her race, the author inserts bits of **hyperbole** and **personification**:

- "I prayed earnestly that I'd be allowed to sit under the house and have the building collapse on my left jaw."

- "I had frozen to the pain, my family nearly had to tie me down to take the toothbrush away."
- ". . . the pain was my world, an aura that haloed me for three feet around."
- "If one was dying, it had to be done in style if the dying took place in whitefolks' part of town."
- "How could one or two or even a mouthful of angry tooth roots meet a wagonload of powhitetrash children, endure their idiotic snobbery and not feel less important?"

A greater **irony** rests on the fact that, during the Depression, Annie Henderson served as unofficial small business loan officer to blacks and whites. Because Dr. Lincoln was one of the recipients of her largesse, she expects a reciprocity that he is unwilling to provide. Not only must she identify herself with the disrespectful use of her first name and endure the haughty white attendant's shutting the door in her face, she must counter her granddaughter's degradation and dehumanization when the dentist sneers, "I'd rather stick my hand in a dog's mouth than in a nigger's." In the aftermath, Annie takes some of the sting from the incident by glorying in her modest retribution—the extortion of ten extra dollars in purported interest.

The fantasized version of the **dialogue** that Maya concocts to salvage her family's pride expands the **motif** of hyperbole:

- "When you get settled in your next place, you will be a vegetarian caring for dogs with the mange, cats with the cholera and cows with the epizootic."
- ". . . she waved her handkerchief at the nurse and turned her into a crocus sack of chicken feed."

In Maya's mind, Grandmother Henderson looms all-powerful, even supernatural—capable of neutralizing the ugliness that exists in the real world. As Maya concludes, "I was so proud of being her granddaughter and sure that some of her magic must have come down to me." The poignant truth is that, for all Annie Henderson's land ownership, shrewd business acumen, and philanthropy toward Stamps's citizens of both races and for all her bravado in facing up to Dr. Lincoln and his rude white nurse, the prevailing **atmosphere** of distrust, bigotry, and hatred prevents her from receiving her share of community respect and status. Living on society's fringe, she remains largely unacknowledged, except by her black neighbors, son, and grandchildren.

Angelou, a master of language, strengthens the historic significance of her autobiography with strict attention to **detail**. For example, her narrative features entertainment and trade names from the period. In addition to the list of popularized fictional characters, such as the Green Hornet, Mickey Mouse, the Katzenjammer Kids, and the Shadow, in this chapter she names "Milky Ways, Mounds, Mr. Goodbars and Hersheys with Almonds," "Mum and Cashmere Bouquet talcum powder," and "Greyhound." Likewise, Annie peppers her speech with the **dialect** common to southern blacks, as in "He tole that little snippity nurse of his'n," "I figger," and "I ain't gonna mess around in no niggah's mouth." These touches, like period relics, anchor the narrative in a time and place and provide the **texture** of verbal authenticity.

The maturity of her grandchildren puts an unfair burden on Annie Henderson. After Bailey's close encounter with the decayed corpse, she knows that he faces the "humorless puzzle of inequality and hate." Concealing her motives beneath her "African-bush secretiveness," Annie scrimps to accumulate enough money to return first Maya, then Bailey a month later, to California. The order of their going suggests that Momma worries more about the vulnerability of Maya than that of Bailey.

- **crushed aspirins or oil of cloves**   home remedies applied to an aching tooth or gum.

- **R.O.T.C.**   Reserve Officers' Training Corps, a military body which demands exacting posture and decorum.

- **epizootic**   an epidemic within a herd of animals.

- **crocus sack**   a burlap bag, often called a "croker sack" or a "gunny sack."

- **peckerwood**   worthless, untrustworthy riffraff.

- **Claude Rains, Herbert Marshall and George McCready**   three significant screen actors of the 1930s and 40s. Rains (1889–1967) earned fame early in his career for his performances in *The Invisible Man, Notorious, Robin Hood, The Prince and the Pauper* and *Casablanca*. Herbert Marshall (1890–1966), an urbane British leading man who lost a leg in World War I, starred in *I Was a Spy, The Dark Angel, A Bill of Divorcement*, and *The Little Foxes*. George McCready (1909–73) left banking to act in *Gilda, Paths of Glory*, and *Commandos Strike at Dawn*.

- **D'Artagnan**   one of the heroes of Alexandre Dumas's *The Three Musketeers*.

- **"The Fall of the House of Usher"**   one of Edgar Allan Poe's most dismal tales of horror, which features the theme of premature burial.

- **"blows and scores" ago**   that is, after a protracted history of assaults and retaliations.

- **djinn**   a spirit, or jinni of Muslim lore which, like the supernatural servant in Aladdin's lamp, can be summoned to assist humans.

CHAPTERS 26–29

The trauma of returning to her parents plunges Maya anew into the unsettled business of rape trauma and guilt. The **imagery** of Annie's reunion with Vivian supplies a clear delineation of proper motherhood. On the one hand, Annie is the "large, solid dark hen." Vivian, the lesser of the two mother figures, is the light-toned chick, communicating in "rapid peeps and chirps." In Oakland and out of her milieu, Annie, a stolid, unflinching figure, adjusts well to the multicultural lifestyle while remaining in Los Angeles for six months. Her going, a shattering, but irrevocable announcement to her dependent grandchildren, illuminates Momma's role as primary parent, a role which ends with her return to Stamps.

Realigning family structure in their San Francisco home around Bailey, Vivian, and Daddy Clidell, thirteen-year-old Maya, like other citizens on the west coast in the aftermath of Pearl Harbor, turns her attention to the threat of a Japanese invasion and to the disappearance of Japanese-Americans, who were incarcerated in internment camps, such as Manzanar in north central California, east of Lone Pine. Angelou's commentary on the complex supplanting of Orientals with Southern blacks illuminates the cultural housing patterns as well as the boost to the black image as the wartime economy increased their worth and self-esteem. She makes no apology for blatant opportunism, which allowed blacks to move into the vacated businesses of Japanese-Americans without qualms.

Like the rest of the new arrivals, Maya develops a sense of belonging to the ten-square-block area around Post Street and evolves the San Francisco personality—friendly, cool, and distinguished. However impressed she is with her new-found freedom and the offerings of a cosmopolitan city, she maintains a sense of racial separation, particularly from white insiders who think of the Southern influx, both white and black, as "raucous unsophisticated provincials." The racial incident that concludes Chapter 27 is one of the rare instances in Angelou's prose which fails to ring true, as though she tacked it on just for effect. An example of **bathos**, or anticlimactic sentimentality, it lessens her skillful recreation of wartime San Francisco. For good reason, she seems to distance herself from the story's origins.

In contrast to this lapse is the extended anecdote which concludes Chapter 29, the San Francisco segment of Maya's education. The **exemplum,** or detailed story of how Red Leg and Just Black bilk a bigoted cracker, a standard version of the trickster motif common to Afro-American and Native American lore, serves a structural purpose. At the end of the narrative, Angelou attempts to rationalize why "It's all right if we do a little robbing now" to even out the balance of years of injustice. Shifting to her own ability to shuck off standard grammar for **vernacular**, she concludes good-naturedly, "It be's like that sometimes." The implication that she learns much about life from the underworld members brought home by Daddy Clidell figures significantly in **sequels** to *I Know Why the Caged Bird Sings*, particularly *Gather Together in My Name*.

- **Capistrano**   a city in Orange County, California, and the location of the ruins of Mission San Juan Capistrano, dedicated in 1776 by Father Junipero Serra, where legend declares the swallows nest each year from March 19 to October 23.

- **Southern Pacific Mole**   a local train which passes through tunnels in Twin Peaks, two hills in central San Francisco.

- **restaurant cum gambling casino**   a combination restaurant and gambling casino.

- **Fillmore District**   the traditional black district in central San Francisco.

- **Nisei**   second generation Japanese-American citizens, or sons and daughters of Japanese immigrants.

- **Axis agent**   a spy for the combined enemy, consisting of Germany, Italy, and Japan, the Axis powers.

- **Pride and Prejudice**   Angelou is making a pun on the title of Jane Austen's novel.

- **Iwo Jima** a volcanic island south of Tokyo, Japan, and the site of a costly battle by American Marines in February, 1945.

- **House Un-American Activities** a committee of the U. S. House of Representatives convened to eradicate fascists, communists, or other un-American infiltrators through intimidation, public disclosure, or imprisonment.

- **Basil Rathbone** captivating British actor (1892–1967) who starred as Sherlock Holmes in *The Hound of the Baskervilles* and *The Adventures of Sherlock Holmes* and had major roles in *Captain Blood, David Copperfield, The Last Days of Pompeii*, and *A Tale of Two Cities*.

- **Bette Davis** two-time Academy Award-winning American actress (1908–89) who starred in *All This and Heaven Too, Jezebel, Dark Victory, The Little Foxes*, and *All About Eve*.

- **arabesque** an elegant ballet pose in which one arm extends forward and the other arm or a leg extends gracefully to the rear.

- **post-Earthquake affair** a house built after the catastrophe which struck San Francisco on April 18, 1906, leaving 700 dead and blocks of buildings collapsed, burning, or uninhabitable. Many of the replacement buildings contained architectural features which were designed to prevent future earthquake destruction, such as huge bolts and stabilizing bars.

- **mark** the unsuspecting victim of a hoax, or con game.

- **C.C.C.** a relief program initiated by President Franklin Roosevelt in 1933 which utilized two and a half million young men for conservation and refor-estation projects.

- **drag** disparage, or denigrate.

- **go down on** suffer a setback or defeat.

- **Lucullan feast** lavish or extravagant entertainment, after the manner of Lucius Lucinius Lucullus (110–57 B.C.), a Roman consul and contemporary of Julius Caesar.

CHAPTERS 30–32

As Maya approaches maturity, she becomes more aggressive, more willing to take risks to establish her autonomy. The set-to with Daddy Bailey's live-in girl friend is one of the liberating elements of the final chapters of *I Know Why the Caged Bird Sings*. Maya's large, awkward frame and lack of refinement contrasts with Dolores's arrogance, daintiness, and fastidiousness; clearly, Maya is destined for trouble in the confines of the trailer that houses the three of them. She competes both consciously and unconsciously for Daddy Bailey's approval, pleasing him with her ability to converse in Spanish and her flexibility and graciousness on the doomed trip to the outskirts of Ensenada. Bailey, aware of the battle for his attention, laughs in self-congratulatory amusement. Dolores, whom Maya characterizes as "mean and petty and full of pretense," is oblivious to the sadistic delight Bailey takes in pitting female against female.

Suspecting shady motives after Bailey deserts her temporarily at the cantina, Maya, unaware that he is off getting drunk with a local woman, fears that she has been bartered as a bride to a border guard. Her frank appraisal of Bailey's egocentric character and dubious principles suggests a destructive inadequacy in the man who should be a major figure in her life. As her mind toys with her father's affront to his only daughter, she bursts into hysterical tears, which Angelou characterizes with **serio-comic** precision. Ridiculing her reputation for brilliance, Maya gamely sets out to drive the fifty descending miles to Calexico.

Following the contretemps with local police, Maya faces greater uproar after Bailey's self-absorption and insensitivity goads Dolores to desperation. His hypocrisy in concealing the fracas to protect his position as "a Mason, an Elk, a naval dietician and the first Negro deacon in the Lutheran church," indicates that he is more concerned with social appearances than with Maya's discomfort, terror, and possible complications from the stab wound. In contrast, Maya, remembering the Baxter family's quick dispatching of Mr. Freeman and fearful of a second eruption of family vengeance, chooses to keep her wound secret from Vivian and to trust native survival skills by running away. Her choice, which is appropriate to teen logic, relieves her tensions and accords some temporary autonomy, which her wounded pride sorely needs.

Bolstered by a lack of parental restraint, like a "loose kite in a gentle wind floating with only my will for an anchor," Maya sleeps away her fears in a junked car and awakens to a multiracial group of other teenage runaways as independent as she. Together, she and the gang enjoy the illusion of total freedom while cadging free baths at one gang member's house. Crediting the experience with initiating her "into the brotherhood of man," she gains new insight into tolerance and trust. Back in San Francisco, believing that she has discredited Dolores's assertion that her mother is a whore, Maya—her displacement at an end—sinks into the satisfaction of costly gains achieved on the way to womanhood.

- **Jane Withers** Atlanta-born actress (1927–) who, from age six, has starred in movies, television, and commercials.

- **Donald O'Connor** musical comedy actor and dancer of stage, screen, and television (1925–) who starred in *Singin' in the Rain*, *No Business like Show Business*, and *The Donald O'Connor Show*.

- **pedal pushers** pants extending to mid-calf length.

- **coq au vin** chicken in wine sauce.

- **prime ribs au jus** beef ribs served with natural juices.

- **cotelette Milanese** chicken breast cutlets dredged in egg, grated Parmesan cheese, and crumbs and braised in butter.

- **pollo en salsa verde** chicken in green chili sauce.

- **enchilada con carne** a tortilla wrapped around a meat filling and topped with chili sauce.

- *mercados* Mexican grocery stores.

- **Pancho Villa** colorful Mexican bandit (1878–1923).

- **Tyrone Power** dark-eyed romantic lead (1913–58) who starred in *The Razor's Edge*, *Captain from Castile*, and *Jesse James*.

- **Dolores Del Rio** fine-featured Mexican actress (1905–83) who starred in *Madame DuBarry* and *Cheyenne Autumn*.

- **Akim Tamiroff** eccentric-looking Russian character actor (1899–1972) who earned an Oscar nomination for his portrayal of Pablo in *For Whom the Bell Tolls*.

- **Katina Paxinou** coarse-featured Greek-born film actress (1900–73) who won an Oscar for her role as Pilar in *For Whom the Bell Tolls*.

- *adios* goodbye.

- *bonita* pretty.

- *esposita* little bride.

- *cantina* saloon.

- *"Cómo está usted?"*   How are you?

- **Zapata**   Mexican revolutionary (1878–1919).

- **la niña**   little girl.

- *"Dónde está mi padre?"*   Where is my father?

- **paisano**   peasant.

- *"Dónde vas?"*   Where are you going?

- **señoritas**   young, unmarried women.

- **Cisco Kid**   dashing Mexican "Robin Hood" character in Western movies, radio, an early television series, and a 50s comic strip.

- **the Fates**   characters in Greek mythology who determined the course of human life.

- *"Si, si"*   Yes, yes.

- *"Gracias"*   Thanks.

- **St. Vitus Dance**   a chronic spastic twitch of face and limbs.

- *risco de Mexico*   Mexican cliff, or crag.

- *"Pasa"*   Pass.

- *policías*   police officers.

- *"Borracho"*   drunk.

- *"Quién es?"*   Who is this?

- *"Mi padre"*   My father.

- *Pobrecita*   Poor little thing.

- *"Qué tiene? Qué pasa? Qué quiere?"*   What do you have? What's happening? What do you want?

- **"The moving finger writes and having writ, moves on . . ."**   a verse from Omar Khayyám's *Rubaiyat* which implies that fate is impervious to human wishes.

- **Lester Young**   innovative tenor saxophonist (1909–59) for Count Basie.

- **Brobdingnag**   a country in Swift's *Gulliver's Travels* that is inhabited by giants twelve times the size of humans.

- **ad hoc**   makeshift; improvised.

- **turned to**   got busy (in this case, preparing food).

CHAPTERS 33–36

More strides toward independence bring Maya closer to self-knowledge. Parallel urges drive Bailey into irreconcilable conflict with Vivian. Maya's impotence to intercede impels her to seek an outside job to escape the misery of a home without Bailey. The **set piece** that plays out between Maya and the Market Street Railway Company receptionist demonstrates a new *savoir faire* in Maya, who denies to be brushed off by mere racism. With a surprising show of charity, she accepts the receptionist as a fellow victim of racism, which refuses employment to black applicants.

The tour de force of becoming San Francisco's first black trolley conductor fails to quell Maya's yearning for some kind of success and proof of womanhood. The decision to mate with a neighborhood boy ends "youth's vague malaise" and leaves her pregnant after a single intimacy. Trusting to faulty logic ("if I could have a baby I obviously wasn't a lesbian") and deception, she weathers impending motherhood alone in a state of denial, "in which days seemed to lie just below the water level, never emerging fully." The eventual bonding with her three-week-old son produces a satisfaction that she has sought throughout her bumpy adolescence.

- **zoot suits**   flashy, disproportionate men's fashions of the early 1940s featuring oversized shoulder pads, thigh-length jackets, and drastically narrowed pants.

- **sloe gin**   a fad drink of the early 1940s composed of grain alcohol flavored with the rosy, sweet fruit of the blackthorn.

- **Count Basie, Cab Calloway, Duke Ellington**   major black musicians of the Big Band era.

- **entangled in the Oedipal skein**   ensnared in a psychological complex, which Sigmund Freud described as an unconscious attraction between mother and son. He based his term "Oedipus complex" on Oedipus, king of Thebes in Greek mythology, who inadvertently kills his father and marries his mother, sires children, then blinds and exiles himself for his crimes.

- **open sesame**   a foolproof method, derived from the magic command that opens the door to the robbers' lair in *Ali Baba and the Forty Thieves*.

- **pavane**   a slow, stately dance.

- **taking low**   being humiliated or berated.

- **in alum drops**   that is, bitterly.

- **claque**   a person, or persons, hired to applaud a theater or opera performance or an actor.

- **en garde**   a fencing term indicating that opponents have taken their places for a duel.

- **inferno dwelling**   that is, living through the childhood hells of humiliation, hate, and abuse.

- **like Hamlet and Laertes**   in the final scene like the conclusion to Shakespeare's tragedy in which neither party survives the duel.

- **gray rococo façades housed my memories of the Forty-Niners, and Diamond Lil, Robert Service, Sutter and Jack London**   the ornate surroundings call up memories of San Francisco's post-Gold Rush heyday, when Diamond Lil earned fame for saloon performances and writers like Robert Service and Jack London preserved the atmosphere in **picaresque** poems, stories, and novels such as "The Cremation of Sam McGee," "The Shooting of Dan McGrew," *Songs of a Sourdough*, *Tales of the Fish Patrol*, and *Martin Eden*.

- **aphorisms**   short statements of wisdom, such as "God helps those who help themselves."

- **cat's ladder**   an intricate web, like the finger games children play with a looped string.

- **Rorschachs**   ink-blot tests which utilize respondents' interpretations of unstructured shapes to diagnose their mental states.

- *The Well of Loneliness*   Radcliffe Hall's 1928 novel about lesbianism.

- **libido**   sex drive.

- **hermaphrodite**   a person born with both male and female sex organs.

- **crabs**   body lice that live in the pubic area.

- **dykes and bulldaggers**   slang terms for aggressive lesbians.

- **Richard Arlen**   character actor (1898–1976) who played in *Man from Montreal, Dangerous Game, Mutiny in the Arctic*, and *Men of the Timberland*.

- **Veronica Lake**   blond film actress (1919–73) made famous in the 1940s for a hairstyle that concealed one side of her face. She appeared in *This Gun for Hire, Hold that Blonde*, and *The Blue Dahlia*.

- **V-Day**   V-J Day, August 15, 1945, celebrating victory over Japan and marking the end of the Pacific phase of World War II.

CRITICAL ANALYSIS

FORM

I Know Why the Caged Bird Sings, Maya Angelou's first venture into **autobiography**, is, like the author herself, packed with promise. Like most autobiography, the story line follows the author's memories, which are colored by photos, letters, and other people's interpretations and repetitions of past **events**. The conversations are obviously padded or wholly fictionalized to fill in what people probably said at the time. The **Maya character**, sometimes endowed with more sophistication and understanding than is appropriate to her young age, reflects a blend of memory and the adult author's hindsight.

Taking her text from a line that echoes through Paul Laurence Dunbar's poem "Sympathy," Angelou selects an evocative **title** linked to images of powerlessness and defeat, but resonant with hope, creative energy, and zestful savvy. As evidence that she has experienced the prototypical struggle for freedom and self-worth, she gives the impression of confessing all triumphs and shortcomings, even scenes and events which a more discreet author might have concealed from public view. The positive **tone** of her work uplifts the reader with renewed belief in the human ability to mitigate random injustice in order to survive. By growing stronger than the challenges that beset her, Maya completes the **coming-of-age pilgrimage** and arrives at adulthood, her dignity intact and her promise assured.

Ironically, the focal point of Angelou's talent is her delight in language, which she masters despite a year's self-imprisonment in muteness. Her skill at interweaving varied sounds, diction, metaphor, verse, hymns, scripture, and rhythms enlivens the narrative with texture and spirit. The resulting facile, readable blend covers the fourteen years of her childhood—from her arrival in Stamps, Arkansas, in 1931 at age three to her graduation from Lafayette County Training School and subsequent bonding with her three-week-old son at her mother's house in San Francisco in October 1945. Examples of her appealing turns of phrase are plentiful:

Anecdote
- There was a cracker in Tulsa who bilked so many Negroes he could set up a Negro Bilking Company.

- I kept my face blank (an old art) and wrote quickly the fable of Marguerite Johnson, aged nineteen, former companion and driver for Mrs. Annie Henderson (a White Lady) in Stamps, Arkansas.

Repartee

- "Hey, baby. What's the news?"
  "Everything's steady, baby, steady."
  "How you doing, pretty?"
  "I can't win, 'cause of the shape I'm in."

Humor

- [Momma] used to add, with a smirk that unprofane people can't control when venturing into profanity, "and wash as far as possible, then wash possible."
- . . . Oh Mizeriz Coleman, how is your son? I saw him the other day, and he looked sick enough to die. . . . From the Uglies.

Biblical Exhortation

- On the other side of Jordan, there is a peace for the weary, there is a peace for me.
- Putting [his teeth] in his pocket, he gummed, "Naked I came into the world, and naked I shall go out."

Memoir

- We learned the times tables without understanding their grand principle, simply because we had the capacity and no alternative.
- On Sunday mornings Momma served a breakfast that was geared to hold us quiet from 9:30 A.M. to 3 P.M.

Conversation

- "They have, in the North, buildings so high that for months, in the winter, you can't see the top floors."
  "Tell the truth."
  "They've got watermelons twice the size of a cow's head and sweeter than syrup. . . . And if you can count the watermelon's seeds, before it's cut open, you can win five zillion dollars and a new car."

Naturalistic Detail

- The sounds of the new morning had been replaced with grumbles about cheating houses, weighted scales, snakes, skimpy cotton and dusty rows.

- Whores were lying down first and getting up last in the room next door. Chicken suppers and gambling games were rioting on a twenty-four-hour basis downstairs.

Philosophy

- The Black female is assaulted in her tender years by all those common forces of nature at the same time that she is caught in the tripartite crossfire of masculine prejudice, white illogical hate and Black lack of power.
- I find it interesting that the meanest life, the poorest existence, is attributed to God's will, but as human beings become more affluent, as their living standard and style begin to ascend the material scale, God descends the scale of responsibility at a commensurate rate.

SETTINGS

The variety of locales emphasizes Maya's ability to thrive, whether in the rural, Depression-era South, St. Louis, San Francisco, southern California, or Mexico.

- Thrust into the threadbare black ghetto of **Stamps** in 1931, she empathizes with the black substrata, where laborers, fearful of intrusive whites and clinging to Bible-based promises, struggle for survival wages:

  Brought back to the Store, the pickers would step out of the backs of trucks and fold down, dirt-disappointed, to the ground. No matter how much they had picked, it wasn't enough.

- In **St. Louis**, far from Stamps's backwardness and religiosity, young Maya, bombarded by a titillating, racy newness, studies the contrasts:

  The Negro section of St. Louis in the mid-thirties had all the finesse of a gold-rush town. Prohibition, gambling and their related vocations were so obviously practiced that it was hard for me to believe that they were against the law.

- The change, which lasts only a year, ends abruptly. One day—without explanation—the traumatized eight-year-old Maya and her brother Bailey are on the train going back to Stamps, where the "barrenness was exactly what I wanted, without will or consciousness."

After achieving partial reprieve from the guilt of Mr. Freeman's death, Maya, threatened by violence, as depicted in Bailey's bug-eyed viewing of a bloated corpse pulled from a pond and lodged in the local jail, is taken to California by Momma, moved from Los Angeles to Oakland and finally to San Francisco's Fillmore district.

- Enthralled with **San Francisco**'s cultural mix, she exults:

  The Japanese shops which sold products to Nisei customers were taken over by enterprising Negro businessmen. . . . Where the odors of tempura, raw fish and *cha* had dominated, the aroma of chitlings, greens and ham hocks now prevailed.

As maturity and a boost in self-esteem work their magic, Maya nests in San Francisco's freedom, gradually turning it into home.

- On a brief vacation in southern California, she envisions visiting Daddy Bailey at a "manor house surrounded by grounds and serviced by a liveried staff." The letdown of seeing his cramped trailer, where family squabbles penetrate frail inner walls, returns her from fantasy to reality. A day trip to **Ensenada** in Bailey's bulky Hudson plunges Maya into a Mexican milieu as poor as Stamps, yet blatantly festive in honor of her father's arrival. On first glimpse, she reports:

  We pulled up in the dirt yard of a cantina where half-clothed children chased mean-looking chickens around and around. The noise of the car brought women to the door of the ramshackle building but didn't distract the single-minded activity of either the grubby kids or the scrawny fowls.

- Later, in an escape from a confrontation with Bailey's mistress and from fear of retribution for the wound in her side by her fierce, relentless Baxter kin, she beds down in a wheelless, rimless "tall-bodied gray car" and spends a month in a **junkyard** on her own.
- Having satisfied her curiosity about life in a teen commune, she returns to the security of Vivian, Daddy Clidell, and **San Francisco**.

  Undergirding these enthralling and sometimes picaresque adventures are **humanistic themes,** each pertaining to some personal fault or social lapse which inhibits Maya's self-fulfillment. These broad ideas

- **self-worth**
- **security**
- **individuality**

suffuse the narrative with significance that is at times poignant and, at others, triumphant. Crucial epiphanies, or coming to knowledge, such as the yard incident in which Maya draws the heart in the dust to honor her grandmother or the night that the family hides Uncle Willie in the vegetable bin to protect him from racist violence, highlight the speaker's pilgrimage toward understanding. The reader, impelled to detest a racist white dentist who would rather treat a dog than relieve the suffering of a black patient, to decry brutal child abuse compounded with guilt and alienation from family, and to cheer a spunky teenager who refuses job discrimination, is likely to identify with and admire a transcendent Maya, who looks within for the way out of racial and patriarchal bondage.

STYLE

I Know Why the Caged Bird Sings underscores meaning through the stylistic **details** that illuminate its themes and action. Angelou utilizes literary devices to emphasize scenes and conversations which reveal the foibles of her characters. For example:

Characterization
- . . . when she was called upon to sing, [Momma] seemed to pull out plugs from behind her jaws and the huge, almost rough sound would pour over the listeners and throb in the air.
- Hence the janitor who lives in one room but sports a robin's-egg-blue Cadillac is not laughed at but admired, and the domestic who buys forty-dollar shoes is not criticized but is appreciated.

Hyperbole
- Sympathy is next to shit in the dictionary, and I can't even read.
- She had the grace of control to appear warm in the coldest weather, and on the Arkansas summer days it seemed she had a private breeze which swirled around, cooling her.

Symbol
- Just my breath, carrying my words out, might poison people and they'd curl up and die like the black fat slugs that only pretended. I had to stop talking.

- [Bailey] said I was quite brave, and that was my cue to reveal our confrontation with the peckerwood dentist and Momma's incredible powers.

Similes
- I was called Old Lady and chided for moving and talking like winter's molasses.
- [Bailey] smelled like a vinegar barrel or a sour angel.

Motifs
- During these years in Stamps, I met and fell in love with William Shakespeare. He was my first white love.
- Stamps, Arkansas was Chitlin' Switch, Georgia; Hang 'Em High, Alabama; Don't Let the Sun Set on You Here, Nigger, Mississippi; or any other name just as descriptive.
- I could cry anytime I wanted by picturing my mother (I didn't quite know what she looked like) lying in her coffin.
- [Bailey] was away in a mystery, locked in the enigma that young Southern Black boys start to unravel, start to try to unravel, from seven years old to death.

Alliteration
- I mastered the art of crocheting and tatting, and there was a lifetime's supply of dainty doilies that would never be used in sacheted dresser drawers.
- The time crowded together and at an End of Days I was swinging on the back of the rackety trolley, smiling sweetly and persuading my charges to "step forward in the car, please."

Sense Impressions
- The odors of onions and oranges and kerosene had been mixing all night and wouldn't be disturbed until the wooded slat was removed from the door and the early morning air forced its way in with the bodies of people who had walked miles to reach the pickup place.
- I sliced onions, and Bailey opened two or even three cans of sardines and allowed their juice of oil and fishing boats to ooze down and around the sides.

Biblical Allusion
- My pretty Black brother was my Kingdom Come.
- The laws were so absolute, so clearly set down, that I knew if a person truly wanted to avoid hell and brimstone, and being roasted

forever in the devil's fire, all she had to do was memorize Deuteronomy and follow its teaching, word for word.

Literary Allusion
- Momma and other ladies caught him in time to bring him back to
  the bench, where he quickly folded upon himself like a Br'er Rabbit
  rag doll.
- My pity for Mrs. Cullinan preceded me the next morning like the
  Cheshire cat's smile.

Aphorism
- "Thou shall not be dirty" and "Thou shall not be impudent" were
  the two commandments of Grandmother Henderson upon which
  hung our total salvation.
- Can't do is like Don't Care.

Parallel Construction
- We danced the jitterbug to Count Basie, the Lindy and the Big Apple
  to Cab Calloway, and the Half Time Texas Hop to Duke Ellington.
- A pyramid of flesh with the whitefolks on the bottom, as the broad
  base, then the Indians with their silly tomahawks and teepees and
  wigwams and treaties, the Negroes with their mops and recipes and
  cotton sacks and spirituals sticking out of their mouths.

Dialect
- Naw, Helen, you ain't standing like her. This here's it.
- Bah Jesus, I live for my wife, my children and my dog.
- Ritie, don't worry 'cause you ain't pretty. Plenty pretty women I
  seen digging ditches or worse.

CRITICAL ESSAYS

WOMEN IN THE MAYA CHARACTER'S LIFE

The montage of female role models in Maya's life significantly
influence her growth and emotional well-being. From early times, she
relies on the stiff, unyielding sanctimony and firm discipline of
Momma Henderson, who insists on clean feet, respectful words,
unquestioning obedience, and hard work. Unable to voice her love
and devotion to Bailey and Maya, Momma settles for wholehearted
attention to their needs, including home cooking, homilies, dental

care, supervised homework, and tailored hand-me-downs or new garments sewn from her chest of fabrics kept safe with mothballs. When the time comes to restore the children to their parents, Momma stoically makes the decision, barters for rail tickets, and accompanies Maya to Los Angeles, where Vivian reassumes the role of mother long enough to get Momma and Maya settled, then returns to San Francisco. Six months later, with no more sentiment than she expressed in Stamps, Momma takes her leave, seemingly content that she has done her best for her youngest grandchild.

Moved to Oakland by Vivian, Maya passes into her mother's wide-open world, where an impromptu party at 2:30 A.M. seems in character with the urbane and much beloved woman who dances the Suzy Q, Time Step, and Snake Hips, bakes biscuits, swears, plays pinochle and poker for a living, and, when the occasion arises, conceals a .32 pistol in her skirt pocket for later use. Disdainfully proud and honest about her lifestyle, Vivian declares that she "wouldn't bust suds for anybody nor be anyone's kitchen bitch." Her yearning for fun and her intense loyalty to the children from whom she lived apart for nearly a decade endear her to Bailey and Maya, who attach no wrong to the spirited Mother Dear, the **foil** of their faithful, predictable Momma.

On the edge of the parental motif, Grandmother Baxter, less of a role model, yet not without influence on Maya, struts her tyranny over precinct favorites during her tenure in St. Louis. After Maya's testimony against the villainous Mr. Freeman, Grandmother Baxter declares the matter at an end by banishing "that evil man's name" from her house. Ten years later, sharing a bed with Maya in Oakland and soothing her nighttime discomfort with deep draws on her "Willies," the cigarettes that deaden her irritated throat with nicotine, she recedes into widowhood and a reduced role in her granddaughter's life.

While coping with the cosmopolitan city of San Francisco, Maya encounters Miss Kirwin, whose professionalism mirrors the aristocratic splendor of Mrs. Bertha Flowers, the Stamps gentlewoman who lifts Maya from her self-imposed sentence of silence by acknowledging her individuality and promise. A maidenly professional, Miss Kirwin, equally interested in developing Maya's considerable intellectual gifts, treats her fairly in the one-sided racial cosmos of George Washington High. Bypassing textbooks, she opens the minds of her pupils to the importance of timely issues and events, leading Maya to an appreciation of "the San Francisco papers, *Time* magazine, *Life* and everything else available to me." In gratitude for the "clean slate" that Miss Kirwin extends to her classes, Maya responds to creative stimulus and returns in later years for visits to the teacher who made a strong, positive impression on her.

Overall, the influence of strong, resolute women permeates Maya's childhood and provides the role models she needs to achieve a self-sustaining dignity. Typical of her hard-headed individualism, however, she exercises an eclecticism over her experiences, editing out the stern hyper-piety of Momma, the sinister power of Grandmother Baxter, the prim scholarship of Mrs. Flowers and Miss Kirwin, and the hedonism and irresponsibility of Mother Dear. Becoming her own woman, Maya demonstrates a hybrid mix of qualities nurtured from childhood and hardened by the struggle. Studying the three-week-old son who mystifies and charms her, she prepares to activate the accrued wisdom that black womanhood has offered.

A NOTE ON SOUTHERN FUNDAMENTALISM

The guiding tenets and rituals of fundamentalism—a twentieth-century religious movement which interprets scripture literally and applies it to daily life—influence Angelou's themes, language, symbols, allusions, and characterizations. A balm to despair and alienation since slave times, soulful worship, plaintive spirituals, and trust in a life in the hereafter bolstered Negroes who were cut off from African faiths by distance, time, and language. Buoyed by post-World War I revivals, which countered growing liberalism, the church found itself perpetually on the defensive and launched sensationalist journals, such as J. Frank Norris's *The Fundamentalist*, against illicit sex, pornography, saloons, divorce, and other embodiments of Satan. A key event in the history of Southern fundamentalism occurred in 1925, when high school biology teacher John T. Scopes, defended by the articulate Clarence Darrow, lost a battle against religious conservatives of Dayton, Tennessee, who, goaded to near-frenzy by populist William Jennings Bryan, sought to supplant Darwin's theory of evolution with biblical creationism in school curricula. Armed with Bibles and muttering amens, the faithful mobbed the courthouse and demanded that their simple interpretation of earth's beginnings was superior to scientific theory.

As a product of the fundamentalist South, Maya, steeped in the uplifting rhythms of spirituals and schooled in scripture, learns early that wisdom is to be found in the Bible, strictly interpreted by Momma and Uncle Willie and dispatched through rigorous **homilies**, some of which (for example, "Waste not, want not") actually derive from sayings by Benjamin Franklin's Poor Richard. In addition to personal prayers, mealtime blessings, and family worship, emotional funerals and flamboyant revivals color the day-to-day milieu of home, work, and school with added reminders of life's grimness and the rewards awaiting the faithful in heaven. Maya internalizes religious strictures, wisely avoiding concepts that strain her young mind and disobeying when natural tendencies override her fear of Momma and her switch. Yet, with all her fundamentalist upbringing, she takes no comfort from the church during her most fearful challenge, the slow recovery from rape.

REVIEW QUESTIONS AND ESSAY TOPICS

(1) Contrast Bailey and Maya Johnson in terms of their coping skills. Make additional contrasts between the older and younger generations, particularly Grandmother Baxter's method of orchestrating her family's murder of a rapist, Momma Henderson's stoicism in the face of three young hecklers, and Vivian's response to being called a bitch.

(2) Explain how and why Vivian and Daddy Bailey seem oblivious to Maya's childhood sufferings and insecurity. Discuss the effects of undeserved exile on both children.

(3) Compare Angelou's depiction of Southern culture with that of Carson McCullers, Eudora Welty, James Agee, William Faulkner, Flannery O'Connor, George Washington Cable, Shirley Ann Grau, Ellen Gilchrist, Paul Green, Zora Neale Hurston, Donald Davidson, and other Southern writers.

(4) Discuss autobiography as an art form. Contrast Angelou's approach to personal narrative with Joy Adamson's *Born Free*, James Joyce's *Portrait of the Artist as a Young Man*, Frederick Douglass's *Narrative of the Life of Frederick Douglass*, George

Orwell's "Shooting an Elephant," Lorraine Hansberry's *To Be Young, Gifted and Black*, Linda Brent's *Incidents in the Life of a Slave Girl*, Maxine Hong Kingston's *Woman Warrior*, John Neihardt's *Black Elk Speaks*, Dick Gregory's *Nigger*, and Anne Moody's *Coming of Age in Mississippi*.

(5) Relate the Maya character's response to rape to current findings about victim dysfunction, loss of speech, refusal to testify, blaming the victim, guilt, irrational fears, and other long-term reactions. Discuss the efficacy of Maya's return to her grandmother and to literature. Explain why the image of the caged bird epitomizes her situation.

(6) Compare the Maya character as protagonist with the fictional Vyry in Phyllis Walker's *Jubilee*, Ruth in Lorraine Hansberry's *A Raisin in the Sun*, O-lan in Pearl Buck's *The Good Earth*, or Celie in Alice Walker's *The Color Purple*. Comment on their victimization by strong or tyrannical male figures and their need for approval and acceptance as women and mothers.

(7) Contrast the film version of *I Know Why the Caged Bird Sings* with other cinematic studies of the rural South, such as *Conrack, Hurry Sundown, Song of the South, Sounder, The Color Purple, Mandingo, Band of Angels, Gone with the Wind, The Foxes of Harrow, Raintree County, Tobacco Road, Pinky, To Kill a Mockingbird, The Autobiography of Miss Jane Pittman*, and *Roots*. Comment on depictions of black/white relationships, particularly over broad economic, educational, and social disparities.

(8) Comment on Angelou's view of women and their ability to cope with poverty, hunger, sickness, rejection, powerlessness, alienation, job discrimination, self-criticism, and social ostracism. Compare her views on female strengths with those in Margaret Mitchell's *Gone with the Wind*, Amy Tan's *Joy Luck Club*, John Steinbeck's *The Grapes of Wrath*, Nathaniel Hawthorne's *The Scarlet Letter* and *The House of the Seven Gables*, Margaret Atwood's *The Handmaid's Tale*, Margaret Craven's *I Heard the Owl Call My Name*, Jeane Houston's *Farewell to Manzanar*, Scott

O'Dell's *The Island of the Blue Dolphins*, Jean Auel's *Clan of the Cave Bear*, and Harriette Arnow's *The Dollmaker*.

(9) Contrast the lifestyle of Stamps, Arkansas, with that of St. Louis, Ensenada, and San Francisco. Comment on opportunities for nonwhites, including the Japanese-Americans who are interned during World War II, women at the cantina near Ensenada, and the pickers who buy supplies at Annie's store.

(10) Supply an overview of the improvement in civil rights from 1930 to the present. List influential nonwhites, particularly sports figures, entertainers, political and religious leaders, inventors and scientists, writers, journalists, and educators.

(11) Discuss cultural influences on Bailey Junior and Maya, especially comic strips, children's and classic literature, sports figures, and religious fundamentalism.

(12) Support or refute Angelou's statement that "every student should be encouraged to read everything in a catholic sense."

(13) Contrast the female characters in *I Know Why the Caged Bird Sings* with those of the poem "Our Grandmothers" from Angelou's *I Shall Not Be Moved*.

(14) Discuss Angelou's comment in *Ebony* magazine in February 1982: "Black people . . . comprehend the South. We understand its weight. It has rested on our backs. We recognize its violence. We have been its victim. We acknowledge its history. It was first written with our blood." Apply her experience to that of other successful black Southerners, such as Andrew Young, Madame Sarah Walker, Dr. Martin Luther King, Jr., Ida Wells-Barnett, James Weldon Johnson, Jesse Jackson, Zora Neale Hurston, Fannie Lou Hamer, Ernest Gaines, Medgar Evers, Mary McLeod Bethune, Margaret Walker, Rosa Parks, Barbara Jordan, and Louis Armstrong.

(15) Explicate William Henley's "Invictus" and Shakespeare's Sonnet 29 and describe their effect on the Maya character. Apply significant phrases to her evolving selfhood. Explain what quality or characteristic causes her to survive and excel.

SELECTED BIBLIOGRAPHY

Angelou's Works

Autobiography

I Know Why the Caged Bird Sings (Book-of-the-Month Club selection, 1970)
Gather Together in My Name (Book-of-the-Month Club selection, 1974)
Singin' and Swingin' and Gettin' Merry Like Christmas (Book-of-the-Month Club selection, 1975)
The Heart of a Woman (1981)
All God's Children Need Traveling Shoes (1986)

Poetry Collections

Just Give Me a Cool Drink of Water 'Fore I Diiie (1971)
Oh Pray My Wings Are Gonna Fit Me Well (1975)
And Still I Rise (1978)
Shaker, Why Don't You Sing? (1983)
Poems: Maya Angelou (1986)
Now Sheba Sings the Song (with artist Tom Feelings, 1987)
I Shall Not Be Moved (1990)

Children's Literature

Mrs. Flowers (1986)

Articles

"My Best Christmas Ever," *Ebony,* December 1987, 35–37.
"They Came to Stay," *National Geographic,* August 1989, 208.
"Nina Simone: High Priestess of Soul," *Redbook*, November 1970, 132–34.
"Cicely Tyson: Reflections on a Lone Black Rose," *Ladies' Home Journal*, February 1977, 40–41, 44, 46.
"Why I Moved Back to the South," *Ebony*, February 1982, 130–34.

Critical Works about Angelou

Afro-American Writers After 1955: Dramatists and Prose Writers. Detroit: Gale Research, 1985.

ANGELOU, MAYA, and CAROL E. NEUBAUER. "Interview," *The Massachusetts Review*, Summer 1987, 286–92.

ARENSBERG, LILLIANE K. "Death as a Metaphor of Self in *I Know Why the Caged Bird Sings*," *College Language Association Journal*, December 1976, 273–91.

BAILEY, HILARY. "Growing Up Black," *The Guardian Weekly*, February 5, 1984, 21.

BAILEY, PAUL. "Black Ordeal," *The Observer*, April 1, 1984, 22.

BANERJEE, SUJATA. "The Many Lives of Maya Angelou," (Baltimore, Maryland) *Evening Sun*, December 14, 1990.

"The *Black Scholar* Interviews Maya Angelou," *Black Scholar*, January-February 1977, 44–53.

"Black Women in the Women's Movement," National Public Radio, 1980.

BLOOM, LYNN Z. "Maya Angelou," *Dictionary of Literary Biography*, Vol. 38. Detroit: Gale Research, 1985.

BLUNDELL, JANET BOYARIN. Review. *Kirkus Review*, October 1, 1978.

BOGLE, DONALD. *Blacks in American Films and Television*. New York: Garland, 1988.

BRAXTON, JOANNE M. "Maya Angelou," *Black Women Writing Autobiography: A Tradition Within a Tradition*. Philadelphia: Temple University Press, 1989, 181–201.

CAMERON, DEE BIRCH. "A Maya Angelou Bibliography," *Bulletin of Bibliography*, January-March 1979, 50–52.

"Candace Awards Presented to Ten Outstanding Blacks During New York Ceremony," *Jet*, August 6, 1990, 14–15.

CHAMBERLAIN, MARY. "Maya Angelou and Rosa Parks," *Writing Lives: Conversations Between Women Writers*. London: Virago, 1988, 1–23.

COLLIER, ANDREA KING. "Poet Finds Completeness in Life's Literature," (Lansing, Michigan) *State Journal*, May 22, 1990.

Contemporary Authors, Vols. 65–68. Detroit: Gale Research, 1977.

Contemporary Authors, New Revision Series, Vol. 19. Detroit: Gale Research, 1986.

Contemporary Literary Criticism, Vol. 12. Detroit: Gale Research, 1979.

VINSON, JAMES, and DANIEL L. KIRKPATRICK, ed. *Contemporary Poets*. New York: St. Martin, 1985.

COSGROVE, MARY SILVA. Review. *Horn Book Magazine*, February 1976.

CRANE, TRICIA. "Maya Angelou: Who Wants to Live in a World Without Courtesy and Humor?" (Los Angeles) *Herald Examiner*, May 25, 1987.

CUDJOE, SELWYN R. "Maya Angelou and the Autobiographical Statement," in *Black Women Writers (1950–1980): A Critical Evaluation*, ed. Mari Evans. Anchor Press/Doubleday, 1984.

DEMETRAKOPOULOS, STEPHANIE A. "The Metaphysics of Matrilinealism in Women's Autobiography," in *Women's Autobiography: Essays in Criticism*, ed. Estelle C. Jelinek. Bloomington: Indiana University Press, 1980, 180–205.

DUDAR, HELEN. "Portrait," *New York Post*, December 26, 1970, 21.

ELLIOTT, JEFFREY M. *Conversations with Maya Angelou*. Fairfax, California: Virago Press, 1989.

_____. "Maya Angelou: In Search of Self," *Negro Historical Bulletin*, May 1977, 694–95.

FEENEY, KATHY. "Maya Angelou," (Tampa, Florida) *Tribune* , October 27, 1989.

GOODMAN, GEORGE, Jr. "Maya Angelou's Lonely, Black Outlook," *New York Times*, March 24, 1972, 28.

GROSSMANN, MARY ANN. "Maya Angelou's Life Is Tough Elegance," (St. Paul, Minnesota) *Pioneer Press-Dispatch*, June 18, 1989.

HITT, GREG. "Maya Angelou: Vibrant Professor-Writer Shares Her Talent, Her Search, Her Self," (Winston-Salem, North Carolina) *Journal*, December 6, 1987.

HOWE, MICHELE. "Angelou's Poetry Builds Bridges between Peoples," (Newark, New Jersey) *Star-Ledger*, June 3, 1990.

JEROME, JUDSON. "Uncage the Songbird," *Writer's Digest*, March 1985, 12–15.

JORDAN, GERALD R. "Angelou Describes Her Life and People," (Philadelphia) *Inquirer*, April 19, 1986.

_____. "Maya Angelou," *New York Daily News*, May 11, 1986.

KENT, GEORGE E. "Maya Angelou's *I Know Why the Caged Bird Sings* and Black Autobiographical Tradition," *Kansas Quarterly*, Summer 1975, 72–78.

KETCHAM, DIANA. "Author Angelou Proves You Can Go Home Again," (Oakland, California) *Tribune*, April 9, 1986.

KOEPPEL, FREDRIC. "Maya Angelou Moves Audience to Cheers," (Memphis, Tennessee) *Commercial Appeal*, July 2, 1991.

LACHTMAN, HOWARD. "Autobiographical Journey Continues," (Palo Alto, California) *Peninsula Times-Tribune*, April 5, 1986.

LEWIS, DAVID LEVERING. "Maya Angelou: From Harlem to the Heart of Africa," *Book World—The Washington Post*, October 4, 1981, 1–2.

LONG, KAREN R. "Maya Angelou Conquers Cleveland—on Her Second Try," Cleveland (Ohio) *Plain Dealer*, May 4, 1986.

LUPTON, MARY JANE. "Singing the Black Mother: Maya Angelou and Autobiographical Continuity," *Black American Literature Forum* 24, Summer 1990, 257–76.

MACKETHAN, LUCINDA H. "Mother Wit: Humor in Afro-American Women's Autobiography," in *Studies in American Humor*, Spring & Summer 1985, 51–61.

"Maya Angelou's Writings Help Touch Hearts of Human Beings of Many Colors," (Newark, New Jersey) *Star-Ledger*, May 11, 1986, n.p.

MCCALL, CHERYL. "Maya Angelou: The Writer-Poet Continues to Find Art in Her Life As She Makes an Emotional Return to Her Native South," *People Weekly*, March 8, 1982, 92, 95–98.

MCMURRY, MYRA K. "Role Playing as Art in Maya Angelou's 'Caged Bird,'" *South Atlantic Bulletin*, May 1976, 106–11.

MCPHERSON, DOLLY A. *Order out of Chaos: The Autobiographical Works of Maya Angelou*. Studies in African and African-American Cultures. New York: Peter Lang, 1990.

MOYERS, BILL. "Creativity," television interview with Maya Angelou for Learning Inc., WNET-PBS, 1982.

NEUBAUER, CAROL E. "Displacement and Autobiographical Style in Maya Angelou's *The Heart of a Woman*," *Black American Literature Forum*, Fall 1983, 123–29.

OLIVER, STEPHANIE. "Maya Angelou: The Heart of the Woman," *Essence*, May 1983, 112–15.

PATERSON, JUDITH. "Maya Angelou," *Vogue*, September 1982, 416, 420, 422.

"Portraits of Black Women: Maya Angelou," (Tampa, Florida) *Tribune,* March 17, 1989, n.p.

RAMSEY, PRISCILLA R. "Transcendence: The Poetry of Maya Angelou," in *A Current Bibliography on African Affairs, 1984*–1985, 139–53.

SHUKER, NANCY. *Maya Angelou.* Englewood Cliffs, New Jersey: Silver-Burdett, 1990.

SMITH, SIDONIE ANN. "The Song of a Caged Bird: Maya Angelou's Quest After Self-Acceptance," *The Southern Humanities Review,* Fall 1973, 365–75.

Something About the Author, Vol. 49. Detroit: Gale Research, 1988.

SOREL, NANCY CALDWELL. "Maya Angelou and Billie Holiday," *Atlantic,* September 1990, 61.

STEPTO, R. B. "The Phenomenal Woman and the Severed Daughter," *Parnassus: Poetry in Review,* Fall-Winter 1979, 312–20.

TATE, CLAUDIA, ed. "Maya Angelou," in *Black Woman Writers at Work.* New York: Continuum, 1983, 1–11.

WASHINGTON, CARLA. "Maya Angelou's Angelic Aura," *The Christian Century,* November 23, 1988, 1031–32.

WESTON, CAROL, and CAROLINE SEEBOHM. "Talks with Two Singular Women," *House and Garden,* November 1981, 128–30, 190, 192.

"Women on Women: Our Past Triumphs Our Future Challenges," *Ladies' Home Journal,* January 1984, 63–65.

Movie Reviews

ARLEN, MICHAEL J. "The Air: The Moon Men," *New Yorker,* May 14, 1979, 157–60.

CRIST, JUDITH. "This Week's Movies," *TV Guide,* April 28-May 4, 1979, A–8.

DAVIS, EARL. "I Know Why the Caged Bird Sings," *Hollywood Reporter*, April 27, 1978.

DOUGLAS, PAMELA. "I Know Why the Caged Bird Sings," *Los Angeles Herald Examiner*, September 2, 1978, B–1, 6.

O'FLAHERTY, TERRENCE. "The Wisdom of Distance," *San Francisco Chronicle*, April 28, 1979.

"Previewed and Recommended," *Los Angeles Weekly*, May 3, 1979.

SHEPPARD, DICK. "Maya Angelou's Caged Bird," *Los Angeles Herald Examiner*, April 28, 1979.

TAYLOR, HOWARD. "She Wants to Change Television's Image of Blacks," *New York Times*, April 28, 1979.

TRESCOTT, JACQUELINE. "Out of the Hostile South Springs a 'Caged Bird,'" *Washington Post*, April 29, 1979.

NOTES

NOTES

NOTES